ALCOHOLISM AND DRUG ABUSE IN THE WORKPLACE

Employee Assistance Programs

Walter F. Scanlon

PRAEGER SPECIAL STUDIES • PRAEGER SCIENTIFIC

New York • Philadelphia • Eastbourne, UK
Toronto • Hong Kong • Tokyo • Sydney

Library of Congress Cataloging-in-Publication Data
Scanlon, Walter F.
  Alcoholism and drug abuse in the workplace.

  Includes index.
  1. Employee assistance programs. 2. Alcoholism and
employment. 3. Drugs and employment. I. Title.
HF5549.5.E42S37 1986   658.3′822   85-19392
ISBN 0-03-005349-8

Published in 1986 by Praeger Publishers
CBS Educational and Professional Publishing, a Division of CBS Inc.
521 Fifth Avenue, New York, NY 10175 USA

© 1986 by Praeger Publishers

6789 052 987654321

Printed in the United States of America on acid-free paper

INTERNATIONAL OFFICES

Orders from outside the United States should be sent to the appropriate address listed below. Orders from areas not listed below should be placed through CBS International Publishing, 383 Madison Ave., New York, NY 10175 USA

Australia, New Zealand
Holt Saunders, Pty, Ltd., 9 Waltham St., Artarmon, N.S.W. 2064, Sydney, Australia

Canada
Holt, Rinehart & Winston of Canada, 55 Horner Ave., Toronto, Ontario, Canada M8Z 4X6

Europe, the Middle East, & Africa
Holt Saunders, Ltd., 1 St. Anne's Road, Eastbourne, East Sussex, England BN21 3UN

Japan
Holt Saunders, Ltd., Ichibancho Central Building, 22-1 Ichibancho, 3rd Floor, Chiyodaku, Tokyo, Japan

Hong Kong, Southeast Asia
Holt Saunders Asia, Ltd., 10 Fl, Intercontinental Plaza, 94 Granville Road, Tsim Sha Tsui East, Kowloon, Hong Kong

Manuscript submissions should be sent to the Editorial Director, Praeger Publishers, 521 Fifth Avenue, New York, NY 10175 USA

For

Mom, Dad, Bro and the Baby

With Love

Preface

Morality, to have any meaning at all, must be a principle of action. It must not be exhortation, sermon, or good intentions. It must be practices.

Peter F. Drucker

The world of work and the world of counseling are not so far apart. Counseling, in fact, has always been a function of supervision, and effective human resource management requires training in both human relations and communications. While technical skills are most important to lower management levels, and conceptual skills are most important to upper management levels, human skills are essential on all levels of management. The ability to work with and understand people is as important to the chief executive office (CEO) as it is to the plant supervisor. Unit chiefs, department heads, division managers, team leaders, vice-presidents, general managers, and frontline supervisors all have one thing in common: they spend a great deal of time communicating, supervising, and negotiating with people. They become quite good at knowing what to say, who to say it to, and when to say it. They are effective observers of people and can quickly assess an environment and determine how to best manage that environment.

People who manage people have an endless flow of problems to solve requiring procedural knowledge as well as good judgment. Any skilled manager or supervisor will know when an employee is not meeting performance standards, but knowing what to do with this information is not always obvious. Some supervisors will go by the book and impose disciplinary measures as per organization procedures while other supervisors might attempt to resolve problems informally. Either or both practices can be employed effectively, depending upon the skill of the supervisor and the structure of the organization. Some problems, however, may call for a different kind of action. Deteriorating job performance resulting from personal problems requires special handling and specific skills. Developing these skills and learning what to do with them are not difficult tasks. An employee assistance program (EAP), among its other functions, provides both training and consultation services for supervisors, and management staff. Most important, the EAP is a resource for the supervisor who has identified a performance problem that might prove to be indicative of a personal problem. Without an EAP such problems may be handled awkardly or not at all. With an EAP in place, however, the solution may be a matter of following procedure. The procedure is, in effect, a cost effective, early intervention management strategy designed to help employees with personal problems that interfere with their ability to function on the job. These problems are more often than not related to the use and/or abuse of alcohol and/or other drugs. The objective is to reduce both the incidence of such problems and the cost of staying in business.

Strategic intervention is, in fact, the focus of this book. In management terms, a strategic control point is where errors are caught before they become serious and expensive problems. This may be any place along an assembly line, any step within the decision-making process, or any point in an employee's work performance. The control point here is, obviously, whenever the employee's performance begins to deteriorate. Realistically, however, intervention is not possible until a pattern of deteriorating job performance is established. The strategy, then, is a timely intervention and referral to the company employee assistance program. This book will provide the reader with an understanding of this strategy as applied to employees whose ability to function on the job has deteriorated because of personal problems.

The term "troubled employee" as used throughout this book means specifically those employees who are identified as employees with alcohol and/or drug problems. This is a departure from the more typical usage where troubled employee could include employees with *any* personal problems. Similarly, "employee assistance program" as used throughout this book means any EAP staffed to work with the chemical-dependent employee whether or not that is the *only* service that the program provides. A program staffed to help only alcohol-dependent employees, for example, will not be referred to as an employee alcoholism program. It will be called an employee assistance program.

The narrower application of these terms serves to eliminate awkward phrases such as "the alcoholism and drug abuse function of the employee assistance program," and/or "the troubled employee suffering from alcoholism and/or drug abuse." In those rare instances where the terms "troubled employee" and/or "employee assistance program" are used in their generic forms, this will be indicated or implicit in the text. In addition, the term "employee assistance program" as used throughout this book does not include, unless otherwise noted, vendors, service centers, or consulting firms contracting with work organizations to provide external EAP services on a fee or retainer basis. External EAPs are a fast-growing service beyond the scope of this book. The book does include, however, a chapter on such services that describes the basic concepts of this alternative to an in-house program.

The concept and practice of employee assistance programming are not limited to the United States. Many work organizations in developed and developing countries have recognized the importance of early identification of the chemical-dependent person in the workplace. The Association of Labor-Management Administrators and Consultants on Alcoholism (ALMACA) has local chapters in several countries, and ALMACA membership includes organizations and individuals from many countries. The research that made this book possible, unless otherwise noted, however, is limited to information collected from sources and studies on programs, organizations, and people in the United States. While much of the information herein might be applicable to organizations in other countries, differences in culture, governmental regulations, and societal mores should be taken into consideration.

The word "corporate" as used throughout this book is applied to any work organization—business, public, or voluntary—where an employee assistance program might be found. The term "corporate setting," therefore, means any organization—business or nonprofit—where people are employed. "Corporation," "organization," "company," "firm," and "work organization" are used interchangeably throughout.

While the terms "drug dependency," "alcoholism," "alcohol dependency," etc. will be used throughout this book without regard to time period, the term "chemical dependency" applies only to those persons who are in the workplace today and those who will be in the workplace in the future. Since "chemical dependency" is a relatively new concept in referring to alcohol and/or drug abusing persons, it will not be used when discussing information of a historical nature. Alcoholism, drug dependency, etc. will be used in those instances.

In researching that information necessary to the discussion on confidentiality, discrimination, and other legal aspects of employee assistance programming, I found that many legal questions were unresolved. I also discovered some contradictions in definitions and interpretations of guidelines and regulations protecting employee and patient rights. In discussing these matters with legal advisers, I was advised to present arguments in general terms and not attempt to solve or resolve these problems. I took their advice. Even experts in the field of employee assistance programming were cautious when discussing what a corporation could do and could not do. A sensitive matter such as screening employees for drug use, for example, was considered by some to be a therapeutic tool and by others to be a violation of civil rights. Organizations using such methods to minimize the use of drugs and alcohol in the workplace emphasized the need for written policies and proven procedures. In terms of legal compliance with guidelines that were less ambiguous, the issue of jurisdiction became a moot point. Compliance with federal and/or local statutes was contingent upon funding, taxes, number of employees, geographical location, etc. With this understanding of the limitations of the legal issues to be discussed, it is hoped that the reader will not apply this information without first conducting research based on his or her corporate or individual situation. The information provided here is intended to provoke thought and open the door to further research.

On the subject of research, the search for information that would eventually make this book possible began in my own small library of books, brochures, bulletins, handbooks, pamphlets, encyclopedias, newspapers, newsletters, periodicals, journals, and reports. The cornerstone of the book is a thesis prepared to fulfill the requirements for Master of Business Administration (MBA) from the New York Institute of Technology.

First I divided the subject of the book into workable segments:

1. The concept of employee assistance programming;
2. The history of employee assistance programming;
3. The history of drug and alcohol use in the United States;
4. Current drug and alcohol use in the United States;
5. The legal, corporate, societal, and individual influences on rehabilitation and employee assistance programming.

Then, after a thorough search and sorting out of the information I had on hand, I used references cited in these works to further my research. The indexes to business and consumer periodicals were included in my search for relevant and timely information, and a computer search by the National Clearinghouses on Drug and Alcohol Information was also conducted.

Primary sources of current information were contacted, such as the National Council on Alcoholism, the Alcoholism Council of New York, the Division of Substance Abuse Services, the Division of Alocholism and Alcohol Abuse, the National Institute on Alcohol Abuse and Alcoholism, the National Institute on Drug Abuse, and the Association of Labor-Management Administrators and Consultants on Alcoholism. Printed and verbal information was secured from these agencies and leads to other sources of information became available. For legal information my primary source of data was the Legal Action Center located in New York City and whatever printed information could be found on the subjects of employee assistance programming and chemical dependency. Personal contacts with managers of employee assistance programs and directors of rehabilitation programs serving work organizations were important primary sources of information.

Finally, both my early personal experience as a "troubled employee" and later as a professional in the field of employee assistance programming provided me the impetus, motivation, and knowledge to write such a book. In 1961 I was fired by a trade publication after several years of deteriorating job performance that was alcohol and drug related. Once unemployed, my chances of recovery diminished and the progression of the illness eventually rendered me unemployable. For the next nine years I remained unemployable, was totally dependent on alcohol and/or drugs, and would be chemical-free only when under lock and key. Had it not been for the countless hospitalizations and institutionalizations, I probably would not be around to tell about it. In one such institution I learned about a program that could help me with my problem. In September of 1969 my recovery began and has continued through today, alcohol- and drug-free since that date. After several years of abstinence, I trained as a counselor and entered the field of alcoholism and drug abuse treatment, eventually moving into program management and finally into the occupational sector and employee assistance programming.

I often wonder what might have happened if the trade publication that I worked for had an employee assistance program. Would I have been referred to such a program and might it have spared me those nine years of degradation and deprivation? For me things turned out well after all, I survived. That was 1961, a time when there were only 50 employee assistance programs in operation nationally. Today there are better than 8,000 such programs, an indication that work organizations are catching on. The chance that a troubled employee will be identified and referred for assistance today is far greater than it was then. This alternative to firing continues to grow, yet many organizations elect not to install EAPs. This book will, hopefully, provide enough information to place the issue in its proper perspective and allow the reader to decide which is the best alternative—termination or intervention. The writer's bias will, inevitably, manifest itself.

Acknowledgments

Many colleagues, associates, and friends, wittingly and unwittingly, made this book possible. Taking an idea and turning it into a readable document is a process requiring the input of many people. This input comes in the form of both hands-on assistance and moral support. It comes directly from those who made contributions in the form of suggestions and criticisms, and indirectly from those whose support and encouragement helped me over the rough spots.

I am especially grateful to the EAP managers, treatment program directors, EAP consultants and personnel managers who contributed their expertise, experience, and time unselfishly so that this effort would be a timely one. Special appreciation goes to the editorial committee of the New York City Chapter of ALMACA Newsletter whose professional and personal support was there when I needed it.

Several people were especially important both to the motivating and writing processes that eventually took on the form of a book. They include Mike Welch whose time spent reviewing drafts spared the prospective reader needless redundancy, and Evan Mason whose sharp sense of organization brought continuity to the manuscript. They also include Evan Leepson whose support and technical direction were always available, and Gerda Steele who provided continuous encouragement and invaluable assistance throughout this project as she has throughout my many projects in the past. The Dogim Group also supported my efforts throughout.

I am particularly indebted to Anita Yulsman who read early drafts and offered comments and suggestions from a layperson's point of view. Her involvement in the project from its earliest beginnings and her encouragement throughout the process deserve special appreciation.

Finally, I thank the faculty of the Center for Business and Management at the New York Institute of Technology including Dr. Marvin J. Weiss, director, and the ten professors who, unwittingly, made this book possible.

Contents

1

The Scope and Cost
of Chemical Dependency

Employee alcoholism and drug abuse are estimated to cost American business and industry billions of dollars each year. A government-sponsored study by the Research Triangle Institute indicates that the cost to the economy for drug abuse alone is nearly $26 billion annually. More than $16 billion of this cost is attributable to lost productivity, absenteeism, medical expenses, disability claims, and theft—corporate expenses that are ultimately passed on to the consumer through taxes and higher prices.[1]

Another study conducted by Croft Consultants, a drug education and counseling firm, placed productivity losses due to drug abuse in the workplace at $17 billion. Croft estimates that there are 4 million workers in the United States abusing drugs to the extent that they have been referred for treatment. According to both government and private-industry figures, the resulting costs to all work organizations is $4,200 per worker, per year.[2]

Yet another study set forth in a special report by the *Harvard Business Review* asserts that the cost of drug abuse to business and industry is $16.4 billion annually. Underscoring the seriousness of the problem, the report concludes:

From the mailroom of the Justice Department to auto assembly plants, the community problems have found their way into the workplace. The use of drugs in the workplace is a serious and growing problem reflecting a national trend, but it is one that business generally ignores.[3]

As for the cost of alcoholism to business and industry, the National Council on Alcoholism sets the figure at approximately $20 billion annually. This figure represents only those losses that are measurable. There are also losses that are not easy to quantify such as the costs of:

1. Poor decision making at all levels of management (which can be greater than all other costs combined);
2. Accidents and injuries;
3. Adverse effects on the morale and performance of co-workers;
4. Work errors;
5. Wasted supplies and materials;
6. Tardiness;
7. "On-the-job absenteeism";
8. Replacement and training.[4]

According to the Industrial Alcoholism Institute, an employee with a drinking problem costs his employer $2,500 per year in productivity losses, absenteeism, and disability benefit claims. Estimating the rate of alcoholism in the workplace to be 10 percent, I.A.I. sets the total cost of corporate alcoholism between $15 billion and $25 billion each year.[5]

A consensus of the various sources published in the past few years suggests that the cost of alcoholism and drug abuse to business and industry is in the neighborhood of $20 billion and $16 billion, respectively. A more recent report by Peter B. Bensinger, former administrator of the Drug Enforcement Administration, however, places the combined costs significantly higher. He reports that the cost of drug and alcohol abuse is $65 billion per year in productivity losses, lives lost, futures forfeited, and unnecessary accidents. While many employers are beginning to recognize the tremendous cost of this growing problem, Bensinger concludes that "More companies must face this problem and provide employee assistance programs to curb substance abuse on and off the job."[6]

Finally, David E. Smith, director of the Haight-Ashbury Free Medical Clinic, put the cost of drug- and alcohol-related workplace problems at $15 billion and $30 billion respectively. These figures, like the rest, represent an estimate of costs and losses to business and industry directly attributed to employee chemical dependency.[7]

Agreement on the actual cost of alcoholism and drug abuse to business and industry is, of course, virtually impossible. The bottom-line figure depends on the many different variables plugged into the formula and the methods employed in the study. Whatever the cost, all agree it is considerable. And the suggestion that the solution must begin in the workplace is, of course, an important one. Chemical dependence, an integrative term coined by the Hazelden Foundation that addresses drugs and alcohol as two sides of the same problem, is a growing concern among corporate managers; and many corporations have responded by implementing employee assistance programs (EAPs) to deal with the problem. Rather than fire employees whose deteriorating job performance is related to a chemical-dependency problem, these corporations are discovering a different solution that is always humanistic and almost always more cost effective than hiring replacements. The cost of rehabilitation for such employees is often less than the cost of training new employees, and certainly less costly than ignoring the problem.

Chemical dependency has reached epidemic proportions. The proliferation of stories and articles in newspapers and magazines across the country is indicative of a serious rather than a casual interest in the subject. And articles in trade publications and business magazines are evidence that drug- and alcohol-related problems are a corporate concern. The all too familiar refrain, "We don't have such problems in this organization," is yesterday's joke. When heard today, it's with tongue firmly implanted in cheek. The problem may be found on all levels of the organization and does not distinguish between men and women. One recent study showed that women, in fact, accounted for one-third of all cocaine users needing treatment.[8] Almost all of these women, like the men, are in the workplace.

Chemical dependency is a social problem. But it is also a corporate problem, a problem that is increasing the cost of staying in business and, more likely than not, affecting the morale of the organization. While it would be unrealistic to believe there is any one solution, the problem can be brought under control. An effective employee assistance program supported by a well-articulated policy on alcohol and drug abuse is the key to this control.

NOTES

1. John Brecher et al., "Drugs on the Job," *Newsweek*, August 22, 1983, pp. 52–60.

2. Peggy Mann, "The Hidden Scourge of Drugs in the Workplace," *Reader's Digest* (February 1984): 45.

3. Peter B. Bensinger, "Drugs in the Workplace," *Harvard Business Review* 60 (November-December 1982): 48–60.

4. William S. Dunkin, *The EAP Manual* (New York: National Council on Alcoholism, 1982), p. 5.

5. "Alcoholism Programs in the Workplace," *Employee Benefit Plan Review* 34 (December 1979): 30, 107.

6. Peter B. Bensinger, "Ways to Stop Drugs," *New York Times*, June 15, 1984, p. 27.

7. David E. Smith speaking at New York conference on "Drugs in the Workplace," sponsored by U.S. Journal Training and The Regent Hospital, March 1985. Material from *Substance Abuse in the Workplace*, ed. David E. Smith, E. Leif Zerkin, and Jeffrey H. Norvey (San Francisco: Haight-Ashbury, 1984).

8. Survey of 800-COCAINE hotline by the Regent Hospital, February-March 1985.

2

Chemical Dependency: The Person, the Definition, the History

WHO IS THE CHEMICAL-DEPENDENT PERSON?

An alcoholic or drug abuser whose comical or tragical behavior immediately identifies the problem is likely to be unemployable, and searching for this person in the workplace would be less than productive. The flask-toting, happy-go-lucky, stereotypic "town drunk" and his drug-shooting counterpart, the romanticized "man with the golden arm" have not worked in years. Those who have managed to hold onto their jobs are a small part of the big problem, and while their problem cannot be ignored, they are the tip of the iceberg.

Many corporate executives and management/supervisory personnel now know this. Government and community efforts to paint a more realistic picture of the chemical-dependent person, and celebrities identifying themselves as recovering chemical abusers, have been important contributions to educating the public. Yet the less enlightened continue to associate the alcoholic with skid row and the drug abuser with violence. Some drug abusers do commit crimes and some alcoholics can be found on skid row, but most are in the mainstream. Only about 3 percent of the problem drinkers are on skid row or have skid-row lifestyles; the remaining 97 percent are living "normal" lives and can be found in the workplace. This fact is not news. Many companies have, in fact, made reference to this in their policies on employee alcohol and drug problems. The Mobil Oil Corporation, for example, addressed the problem of stereotyping in its manual over seven years ago:

One of the chief problems in dealing with alcoholism and drug abuse is the elimination of stereotyping ideas surrounding these conditions. The typical alcoholic is often erroneously conceived of as a skid row derelict. Actually, only a very small proportion of alcoholics fall into this category. Most are average citizens. Many are employed.[1]

As for the drug abuser, even the hard-core street addict is not likely to commit violent crimes. But equally important, this type of drug abuser is in the minority. Less than 600,000 heroin addicts exist in a drug-using population of 35 million Americans.[2] This means that more than 34 million others are using and/or abusing a variety of mood-altering substances! These facts come as no surprise to those professionals responsible for treating chemical-dependent persons. Many corporations, especially those with EAPs in place, are likely to be aware of the impact of these "others" on productivity and job performance. And, as discussed in the literature and in corporate manuals on the subject, these are employees whose prescribed and/or recreational drug use has progressed to the point where their ability to function normally is impaired.

The stereotype of the drug abuser as a hard-core street addict is equally erroneous. The fact is that while the use of heroin has received much public attention, the misuse of certain prescribed medications by the average citizen is the more common drug problem. Physical and psychological dependencies on tranquilizers and stimulants pose health problems very similar to those of alcoholism. Furthermore, it is not uncommon for individuals to develop dual dependencies on alcohol and drugs.[3]

As noted above, this policy was formulated more than seven years ago yet it reflects an enlightened approach to the problem. The chemical-dependent person may be someone who discovered that two valiums are better than one or that the codeine prescribed for a toothache felt good even when there was no pain to kill.

While cocaine and marijuana are not likely to be prescribed by physicians, the abuse of these substances in today's society is not so different from misusing prescribed medications. The availability of these and other mood-altering substances has made recreational drug use as easy as ordering a drink or taking a second valium. The same person, in fact, may order a drink, do a line of coke, smoke a joint, or drop a valium.

THE CHANGING PROFILE

The drug abuser that we are talking about here is different from the one we thought we knew. Unlike the classic heroin user whose progression to the final stages of addiction could take as little as 20 months, or the traditional alcoholic who might survive for 20 years before "hitting the skids," the new chemical-dependent person is likely to fall somewhere in between. The progression here will be less predictable and the profile of this person will defy existing stereotypic notions. The profile, in fact, will be the profile of an executive, a secretary, a manager, a laborer, an office worker, or a telephone repair person. A study was conducted involving 500 randomly selected individuals who called the 800-COCAINE hotline and the following profile emerged:

> A close-up of the 500 shows that they were 30 years old, with a majority aged 25 to 40, at the time of their call to the hotline. Some were as young as 18 and as old as 78. They had begun to use coke just under five years earlier. Contrary to popular belief, cocaine abuse is not strictly a male phenomenon. One out of three of the coke users was a woman. The overwhelming majority (85 percent) was White; the rest were Black or Hispanic. They were well educated, on average having completed just over 14 years of schooling. Within the group there were college graduates, men and women with M.D. and legal degrees, business people, educators, engineering Ph.D.s and airline pilots with years of training to qualify them for their jobs. They averaged about $25,000 a year, and of all those who gave their income, an astonishing one in almost seven earned $50,000 a year or more. Of the 500 respondents, almost two-thirds were living in New York, New Jersey, California and Florida, the rest in 33 other states.[4]

The study also showed that 70 percent of the cocaine users also used alcohol, heroin, and other drugs either with cocaine or after the cocaine-induced euphoria dissipated. Twelve percent admitted they had previously been arrested for dealing cocaine—undoubtedly a small fraction compared to those who deal but have not been arrested. Since a high percentage of the respondents in this survey were employed, it follows that the cocaine user can purchase the drug in the workplace. With a potential market of 22 million who have tried cocaine, and thousands more trying it for the first time each day, the dealer does not have to look far for business. The business is right there in the workplace.

In still another survey of cocaine users, Arnold M. Washton, director of substance abuse research and treatment for The Regent Hospital, reported that the profile of the cocaine user continues to change. It is changing from a person likely to be an educated professional with above-average earnings to one who is less than affluent, middle-class, and working. While there is an increasing number of users and abusers among the working population, equally significant is the fact that there is an increasing number of employees using drugs *while* working. Eighty-three percent of those surveyed admitted to using drugs on the job and 25 percent used drugs on a daily basis at work! This problem is becoming a serious health concern in work organizations throughout the United States.[5]

THE MEDICAL PROFESSION DEFINES
ALCOHOL AND DRUG ABUSE

Managers and supervisors need not know the clinical features and behavioral dynamics of chemical dependency to address the problem in the workplace, yet when conducting training sessions on how to use the company EAP effectively, many such questions are asked. There is a curiosity about the disease concept of alcoholism and about the medical approach to treating drug abusers. Supervisors want to understand the difference between an alcoholic and a heavy drinker as well as the difference between a recreational drug user and a drug abuser. They want to be convinced that chemical dependency is, indeed, a medical problem amenable to treatment before they even consider using the EAP.

While there are as many definitions as there are species of alcoholics, here are some definitions referred to and accepted by the professional community. *The Merck Manual* offers the following:

> Alcoholism is a chronic illness of undetermined etiology with an insidious onset, showing recognizable symptoms and signs proportionate to its severity.

Merck's classification of alcohol dependence divides those who drink into three distinct categories: social drinkers, social alcoholics, and alcoholics.

Social drinkers drink with their friends. Alcohol is a part of their socializing process but not essential, and they do not tolerate disturbing drunkenness. Intoxication among social drinkers is rare; it may occur only during some group activity such as a wedding, wake, or New Year's Eve party where excessive drinking is permitted.

Social Alcoholics, by comparison, are frequently intoxicated but maintain some behavioral controls. They anticipate occasions that require martinis for lunch and routinely expect "a couple" before going home. They avoid bars that feature entertainment and seek those known for generous drinks . . . despite his [her] excessive drinking, he [she] has no "hangover," and his [her] drinking does not disrupt his [her] marriage or seriously interfere with his [her] work. . . .

An *alcoholic* is identified by severe dependence or addiction and a cumulative pattern of behaviors associated with drinking. (1) frequent intoxication is obvious; interferes with ability to socialize and work. Drunkenness may lead to (2) marriage failure and (3) being fired from job (4) driving while intoxicated (5) medical treatment (6) physical injury (7) arrests (8) hospitalization.[6]

Taber's Cyclopedic Medical Dictionary offers a variation on the *Merck* definition:

Alcoholism is a chronic progressive, and potentially fatal disease. It is characterized by tolerance and physical dependency or pathologic organ changes, or both—all the direct or indirect consequences of the alcohol ingested.[7]

"Loss of control" is the characteristic that separates the alcoholic from the nonalcoholic. While some alcoholics may argue that they do not get drunk every time they drink, their inability to *consistently* control their consumption is what makes them different from social drinkers. An alcoholic will have every good intention to leave a bar after a few drinks and go home and may, in fact, succeed on some occasions. But more often than not this willpower will prove no match for the insidious onset of the disease.

While the American Medical Association has recognized alcoholism as a disease since 1956, drug abuse is not classified as such.[8] This is somewhat paradoxical in that alcoholism so classified as a medical problem (disease) is often treated behaviorally, that is, Alcoholics Anonymous, etc., while drug abuse which is often viewed as a behavioral problem (illegal) is treated medically, that is, methadone maintenance, etc. Albeit, *Merck's* definition of drug abuse is as follows:

> Currently, "drug abuse" involves three distinct problems: (1) the experimental and occasional use of drugs by individuals partially because such use is culturally acceptable; (2) psychologically dependent abusers who try to find relief from their problems through drugs or who seek "insight" into their problems via drugs; and (3) the "true addicts" who use drugs for the "high," and once drug-dependent continue to use them to prevent the discomfort of withdrawal.[9]

While this definition separates the drug abuser into three different categories, it could also be viewed as a continuum or progression. The 35-year-old employee who is introduced to cocaine at a party, for example, might continue to use the drug recreationally—for a while. But accessibility of the drug in the workplace could change this "recreational" user into a cocaine abuser, eventually leading to dependence on the substance. Dealing cocaine or stealing money to insure a continuous supply might be expected. This is not to say that every person who uses drugs recreationally will become an addict, but many will experience this loss of control.

Other definitions of alcoholism and drug abuse are more simply stated:

> Alcoholism is a condition which is characterized, among other things, by the drinker's consistent inability to choose whether to drink at all, or to stop drinking when he or she has obviously had enough, and drug abuse is the use of a drug for other than medicinal purposes which results in the impaired physical, mental, emotional or social well-being of the user. Drug misuse is the unintentional or inappropriate use of prescription or over-the-counter drugs, with similar results.[10]

THOSE WHO DO AND THOSE WHO DO NOT

Whichever definition of alcoholism and/or drug abuse one chooses, it would be safe to assume that the chemical-dependent person did not intend to lose control. He or she probably drank or used drugs for the same effect that the social drinker or recreational drug user seeks. The difference between the two, as stated above, is that one can stop at any point and the other cannot. In terms of the progression of chemical dependency, the first drink or use of drugs usually starts in a social setting. It might be at a party, at home, with a group of kids on the corner, or in a school bathroom. It could be a glass of wine, a can of beer, or a marijuana cigarette. For some, the new experience may not be a desirable one, and they are not likely to have another drink or drug until an appropriate occasion arises—if at all. Others may have found the experience pleasurable, the "high" was enjoyable and the altered state of consciousness they experienced was fun. They enjoyed the effect of the chemical but equally important, they also enjoyed the camaraderie that went along with the experience. They were likely to place the experience in its proper perspective and go on to the more important things in their lives.

For most people the first experience with mood-altering chemicals is hardly worth remembering. For others, however, the effect is dramatic. In recalling their first experience with drinking or using other drugs, many recovering chemical-dependent people will say such things as, "It was like magic"; "It made me feel wonderful"; "It was like being born all over again"; "It made me feel that my whole life had changed"; or "I realized how easy it was to feel better than I had ever felt before." With just one drink or drug, most chemical-dependent persons will recall that it became possible to feel attractive, smart, important, witty, and powerful.[11] Conversely, alcoholics drink both to ". . . relieve painful feeling states" and ". . . to manipulate the environment," that is, to relieve the pain of not feeling attractive, important, witty, etc. and to manipulate the environment so as to create the "illusion" that they are.[12] They may, indeed, possess these qualities but do not feel that they do.

Whatever the drug of choice may be—and alcohol is a drug—most chemical-dependent persons will be found in the workplace. People have always used substances to alter their state of consciousness and people have always worked for a living. It is likely, then, that those experiencing a "dramatic" effect when first introduced to drugs or drinks will be working alongside those who placed little importance on the event.

SOCIAL DRINKS AND RECREATIONAL DRUGS ARE HERE TO STAY

Andrew Weil in his 1973 book, *The Natural Mind*, offered a new way of looking at drugs and the higher consciousness. Weil says that the use of drugs to alter consciousness is nothing new, that "It has been a feature of human life in all places on earth and in all ages of history." He goes on to say that the only people lacking a traditional intoxicant are the Eskimos, who had the misfortune to be unable to grow anything and had to wait for white men to bring them alcohol. Alcohol has always been the most commonly used drug simply because it does not take much effort to discover that the consumption of fermented juices produces interesting variations from ordinary consciousness.[13]

Weil argued that there is no evidence that a greater percentage of Americans are now taking drugs than once did, only that the younger Americans are coming to prefer illegal drugs like marijuana and hallucinogens to alcohol. While there is new evidence that more people are using drugs today, a Consumer Union report seemed to support Weil's position at that time. In their study that might now be considered a classic in the field, *Licit & Illicit Drugs*, it was reported that the drug of choice had changed and that, in fact, there were periods in American history where drug use was so common it was hardly considered a problem. Before the turn of the century physicians dispensed opiates directly to patients, drugstores sold them over the counter, and grocery and general stores stocked them on their shelves; drugs could be ordered by mail and there were countless patent medicines on the market containing opium and morphine which were sold under such names as Godfrey's Cordial, Mrs. Winslow's Soothing Syrup, and McMunn's Elixir of Opium.

Cocaine remained popular through this period and into the twentieth century:

> By 1890, the addicting and psychosis-producing nature of cocaine was well understood in medical circles; yet for another twenty years it does not appear to have occurred to many people to demand a law against the drug. In the United States, cocaine was widely used not only in Coca-Cola but also in "tonics" and other patent medicines.[14]

LEGISLATION

Several major steps were taken early in this century to control the distribution and sale of opiates and cocaine in the United States. The first was in 1906 when Congress passed the first Pure Food and Drug Act. This act required that medicines containing opiates and certain other drugs must state such on their labels. The Harrison Narcotics Act of 1914, however, totally cut off the supply of legal opiates for addicts. In 1924 a law was enacted prohibiting the importation of heroin altogether, even for medicinal use.

Both local and federal statutes enacted since the Harrison Narcotics Act were aimed at controlling drug use and abuse in this country. There were also early attempts at treatment, including expensive private sanitariums and federally supported facilities such as Lexington Hospital in Kentucky. Methadone maintenance clinics are a viable treatment approach today, but few people are aware that opiate clinics dispensing heroin and morphine existed between 1912 and 1922.[15]

Widespread use of marijuana is a problem in the workplace today. It is the drug of choice among our youth, but this is not the first time in American history that "smoke" gained popularity. By the 1930s there were more than 500 "tea pads" in New York City alone.[16] Ironically, it was a change in the laws rather than a change in drug preference that stimulated a large-scale marketing of marijuana for recreational use in the United States. The enactment of the Eighteenth Amendment and the Volstead Act of 1920 raised the price of alcoholic beverages and made them less accessible. This fact and the inferior quality of the alcoholic beverages that were available triggered a substantial commercial trade in marijuana for recreational use.[17] As in the buying and selling of any product, the economic laws of supply and demand prevailed. It became cheaper and safer to smoke pot than to drink booze.

Attempts at mandating sobriety and abstinence have had little success. In 1918, four years after the Harrison Narcotics Act was passed, a committee was appointed to look into what appeared to be a growing drug abuse problem. The committee found that illegal drugs, specifically opiates and cocaine, were being used by 1 million people, and the underground traffic in narcotics was about equal to the legitimate traffic. Organized smuggling rings had formed and drugs were entering the United States through sea ports and across Canadian and Mexican borders. Twenty surveyed cities had reported increased drug usage since the passage of the Harrison Narcotics Act.[18]

The Volstead Act did not fare any better. Prohibition, the enforcement mechanism for the Eighteenth Amendment, was impossible to enforce. The benefits of this piece of legislation were overshadowed by its dramatic failures. Room and Mosher note:

In American and intellectual life since Repeal, Prohibition, an attempt at a structural and societal solution to alcohol problems, has been seen as an entirely negative experience, and those interested in alcohol problems and in helping alcoholics have often been concerned to disassociate themselves from the taint of temperance.[19]

Just as the Harrison Narcotics Act turned drug use into a crime, the Volstead Act turned drinking into a crime and created an "industry" for the underworld. While there is some evidence that it decreased alcohol-related problems among the "working class," it created bootlegging, racketeering, and related crimes as well as hypocrisy, a breakdown in government machinery, and a demoralization of private and public life.[20]

TREATMENT

The United States has come a long way since the Harrison and Volstead Acts. While we continue our attempts to control drug and alcohol use through legislation, we also try to control it through education and treatment. There had been many voluntary efforts to address the problem of alcoholism, but the greatest success came when William (Bill W.) Wilson cofounded Alcoholics Anonymous (A.A.) in 1935. This was a pivotal point in treatment history that paved the way for many self-help groups that followed. Narcotics Anonymous, Pills Anonymous (aka Drugs Anonymous), and Cocaine Anonymous are some of the more recent offshoots of that extremely successful organization. Drug-free therapeutic communities (TCs) also got their start indirectly through A.A. In 1958 Charles E. Dederich, a former A.A. member, established Synanon in California as a drug-free treatment center for drug addicts. This was an innovative approach utilizing a powerful encounter component to treat the hard-core drug addict. Other therapeutic communities that followed including Daytop, Phoenix House, Odyssey House, and Project R.E.T.U.R.N. were also structured on the Synanon model. They have since modified their treatment approach to meet the needs of the changing drug culture.

Today there are a vast variety of treatment programs providing a wide range of services. Halfway houses, rehabilitation centers, outpatient clinics, and detoxification programs are located throughout the United States to meet the individual treatment needs of the chemical-dependent person. Structured programs of recovery that provide individual counseling, group therapy, and education are complementing the self-help efforts of Alcoholics Anonymous, Drugs Anonymous, and Narcotics Anonymous. Programs engage families in the treatment process, and self-help groups provide help for spouses, children, and the loved ones of chemical-dependent persons.

Treatment for the chemical-dependent person has become a business. The corporate sector has joined the voluntary and public sectors in providing services. Several health-care chains have 28-day rehabilitation programs and out-patient programs scattered throughout the country that specialize in alcoholism, cocaine abuse, and/or chemical dependency treatment, in general. These new programs offer quality services without compromising the tenets of professional care and effective treatment. They are, in fact, competitive in every way. Their market is the chemical-dependent employee population, and they must show a consistent success rate to insure referrals from the business community.

While legislation is necessary to minimize the availability of illegal substances and to control the consumption of legal drugs, the emphasis today is clearly on treatment and education. As this movement continues, so too will the movement to identify the chemical-dependent person before he or she becomes unemployed and a ward of the community. This early identification can happen, of course, only in the workplace.

NOTES

1. "Alcohol and Drug Abuse Program Manual" (New York: Mobil Oil Corporation, 1978), p. 1. Offset.

2. Jean Seligmann et al., "Getting Straight," *Newsweek*, June 4, 1984, pp. 62–69.

3. "Alcohol," Mobil, p. 1.

4. Mark S. Gold, *800-COCAINE* (Toronto: Bantam, 1984), p. 9.

5. Arnold M. Washton, The Regent Hospital interviewed on radio station WINS New York, March 14, 1985.

6. *The Merck Manual* (Rahway, N.J.: Merck, 1977), p. 1,519.

7. *Taber's Cyclopedic Medical Dictionary* (Philadelphia: F. A. Davis, 1982), p. A-37.

8. *Target: Alcohol Abuse in the Hard-To-Reach Work Force* (Rockville, Md.: National Institute on Alcohol Abuse and Alcoholism, 1982), p. 3.

9. *Merck*, p. 1,505.

10. *Let's Talk About Drug Abuse* (Rockville, Md.: National Institute on Drug Abuse, 1979), pp. 10, 3.

11. Harry Milt, *The Revised Basic Handbook on Alcoholism* (Maplewood, N.J.: Scientific Aids, 1977), p. 22.

12. Sheila B. Blume, "Group Psychotherapy in the Treatment of Alcoholism," in *Practical Approaches to Alcoholism Psychotherapy*, ed. Sheldon Zimberg, John Wallace, and Sheila B. Blume (New York: Plenum Press, 1978), p. 70.

13. Andrew Weil, *The Natural Mind* (Boston: Houghton Mifflin, 1973), p. 17.

14. Edward M. Brecher et al., *Licit & Illicit Drugs: The Consumer Union Report* (Boston: Little, Brown, 1972), pp. 3–7.

15. Ibid., pp. 47–55, 115.

16. David Solomon, "The Marijuana Problem in the City of New York," *The Marijuana Papers* (New York: Bobbs-Merrill, 1966), p. 246.

17. Brecher, *Licit*, p. 410.

18. Ibid., p. 51.

19. Mark H. Moore and Dean R. Gerstein, *Alcohol and Public Policy: Beyond the Shadow of Prohibition* (Washington, D.C.: National Press, 1981), p. 63.

20. Ibid., p. 62.

3

The Corporate Response to Chemical Dependency

THE EAP DEFINED

"Employee assistance programming" is a generic term used to identify any such service that addresses the personal problems of an employee. It is sometimes described as an employee-sponsored employee benefit consisting of diagnostic and referral services for employees and their families. Within any given organization this service may have a different name. It might be called the "Employee Counseling Service," the "Personal Assistance Program," the "Personal Counseling Service," the "Occupational Chemical-Dependency Program," the "Special Medical Services Unit," etc. While most large employee assistance programs are staffed with generalists who can handle a range of personal problems, or have outside resources where employees may be referred for help, some programs are limited in the services they provide. The EAP evolved from the occupational alcoholism program (OAP) concept and many programs continue to provide services only for alcohol and/or drug-dependent employees.

While problems other than alcohol and drug abuse may also affect job performance, the term "troubled employee" as used throughout this book means a chemical-dependent employee, and an "employee assistance program," unless stated otherwise, is any in-house program that addresses this problem. The discussion of services provided for those employees whose job performance is affected by personal problems other than chemical dependency is not within the scope of this book. A brief outline of these services is provided, however, to show the range and the focus that some organizations assume in the design of their program.

While an EAP by definition addresses the problems of employees and their families, a survey of programs across the country shows that some EAPs do more. Many, in fact, could be called "wellness programs" in that the emphasis is on health rather than on problems. A sampling of services offered include problem assessment and diagnosis, in-house counseling for both employee and family members, psychiatric evaluations, family therapy, career counseling, financial guidance, legal advice, social activities, housing referral services, chemical-dependency treatment and/or referral for treatment, and employee education and training on a variety of health-care topics. Other programs do only problem assessment and refer the employee to an outside provider service for assistance. Most programs, however, fall somewhere in between.

Whatever services a program offers above and beyond helping employees to solve problems affecting job performance, the EAP's primary objective should not be compromised. That objective is the effectuation of the organization's policies and procedures on identifying and providing assistance for troubled employees. While the objective is to provide assistance, the goal is to keep the good employee working and free of problems that could affect job satisfaction and performance. Neither the range of services offered nor the program's level of sophistication should interfere with this mandate. The New York Business Group on Health (NYBGH), in fact, describes employee counseling programs as "company policies, procedures and services which identify or respond to employees whose personal, emotional or behavioral problems interfere directly or indirectly with work performance." In a handbook published by NYBGH, EAPs can have any one of three focuses: single-focus, multiple-focus, or comprehensive.[1] At one end of the continuum would be the single-focus providing only one service which could be either information/referral or short-term counseling for alcohol and/or drug abusers. Although it could, conceivably, concentrate its efforts on any one employee problem such as gambling or overeating, its focus is almost always on alcohol abuse and, more recently, chemical dependency. At the opposite extreme would be a comprehensive program offering a range of services provided by a staff of specialists. The scope and size of the program separate it from the multiple-focus program which may have only one staff member. The multiple-focus program will always include alcohol and/or drug abuse services, but it may compromise its potential effectiveness in attempting to do too much with too little.

Employee counseling programs offer employees at all levels of the organization confidential help and/or professional information, care, or referral to appropriate sources of help.[2] The National Council on Alcoholism (NCA) defines any such service simply as "A mechanism for implementing an organization's policy on alcoholism [drug abuse]." NCA goes on to say that the organization's position is set forth in the written statement of policy, and the policy is implemented through written procedures.[3] The New York State Division of Substance Abuse Services (DSAS) offers still another description of an EAP. DSAS identifies it as a ". . . unit within a worksetting focused on reaching out to employees with problems, identifying the problem and assisting in putting that employee in contact with those who can help."[4]

Deteriorating job performance is usually the basis for referring an employee to an EAP. It is then the function of the EAP practitioner to determine what the underlying problem may be. While the majority of referrals turn out to be alcoholism or drug abuse cases, other personal problems can also affect an employee's functioning. Family problems, depression, gambling, or compulsive eating behavior are examples of some such problems manifesting symptoms that may resemble chemical dependency. In organizations that have single-focus rather than comprehensive EAPs, however, the cause of the deteriorating job performance is usually determined *before* the referral is made. If the supervisor refers an employee directly to an alcoholism program, for example, alcohol abuse has already been established. Such a referral is likely to occur only when the employee has a known history of alcoholism or when a company rule has been violated, that is, drinking on the job. The limitation of this model is that it precludes early identification of the chemical-dependent person. If the employee is drinking or using drugs on the job, the problem has already progressed beyond the early stages. Some organizations with single-focus EAPs circumvent this problem, however, by requiring that supervisors stick to job performance and refer troubled employees to the medical department rather than to the *alcoholism* program for an evaluation. Such arrangements work where the EAP is an integral function of the medical department but, more often than not, many such referrals fall through the cracks. This is why "broad-brush" programs—programs that deal with all employee personal problems—are the models that most organizations are developing. Not only does this model keep the supervisor out of the treatment business, but it allows the employee to participate in an "assistance program" rather than an "alcoholism/drug abuse program." This is particularly important when the program's physical location does not guarantee total privacy.

THE EARLIER PROGRAMS

The employee assistance program (EAP) concept practiced today has its roots in the earlier occupational alcoholism program (OAP) model of the 1940s. The evolution of the concept from helping employees with drinking problems to helping employees with *any* personal problems picked up momentum in 1965 when a study by the National Council on Alcoholism (NCA) indicated that programs should focus on job performance rather than on alcoholism symptoms for the purpose of early identification of alcoholic employees.[5] Prior to that time supervisors were expected to watch for behavioral, physical, and social indications of alcohol abuse. They were "trained" to note cutaneous symptoms such as a red nose and to watch for staggering employees and for employees with alcohol on breath.

As stated in Chapter 2, this approach to identifying troubled employees would reveal the tip of the iceberg. The change in technique to a focus on job performance was important in that it served to identify troubled employees early on, often before they began drinking or drugging on the job. But equally important is that this change required the supervisor to function only as a supervisor and not as a diagnostician. Deteriorating job performance, often an early sign of alcoholism or drug abuse, would now be the supervisor's only concern—looking for "drunks" would no longer be a function of the job.

Troubled employees who are identified through this method are then referred to the employee assistance program where an assessment is made, and treatment, if indicated, is planned. While more than 70 percent of such referrals to the EAP would prove to be alcohol problems, the rest, as discussed in the previous section, would be employees with other personal problems, hence the beginning of the "broad- brush" concept of troubled employee identification. When the first formal multiplant programs (OAPs) were soon combined, however, providing industry with a new incentive to deal with this growing concern.

First was the birth and sudden growth of Alcoholics Anonymous (A.A.). Second, influential and dedicated medical directors came to support and actively initiate programs during this period, providing a high status leadership to the emerging programs. Third, this development converged with the unique labor market conditions during World War II.[10]

One report by the National Institute on Alcohol Abuse and Alcoholism (NIAAA) credits E. I. DuPont with the first known multiplant program and Eastman Kodak with the second, both in 1944.[11] Whichever came first, many other organizations, large and small, followed. They included North American Aviation, the Hudson Department Store, the Western Electric Company, the Caterpillar Tractor Company, Thompson Aircraft Products, and the United States Navy.[12] New York Life Insurance Company, Allis Chalmers, and Consolidated Edison later joined the growing number of companies offering help to the alcoholic employee.

EIGHT THOUSAND EAPs NOW IN PLACE

The concept of occupational alcoholism programming had, obviously, taken hold. By 1959 there were 50 major companies with programs in place and by 1973 there were 500 programs nationwide.[13] There are presently 8,000 programs operating in the United States.[14] These programs can be found in virtually every type of organization where people are employed. Local police and fire departments have programs as do airlines, railroads, manufacturing firms, labor unions, suports associations, municipalities, service organizations, and advertising agencies. Smaller companies often group together and form consortiums and others enter into contractual arrangements with EAP consulting firms. Work organizations in the public, private, or voluntary sectors have discovered that EAPs are a very effective approach, and often a very efficient approach, to reducing alcohol- and drug-related job-performance problems.

One study reported that 56.7 percent of the top 1,000 companies listed by *Fortune* had programs aimed at helping alcoholic and drug abusing employees.[15] Another study by the American Society of Personnel Administrators in 1983 noted that 55 percent of all com-

launched in the early 1940s alcoholism was the only concern. W
it is difficult to credit any one company with the first OAP, T
and Schonbrunn named E. I. DuPont de Nemours and Company :
the Eastman Kodak Corporation on the East Coast, and No
American Aviation on the West Coast as ". . . having the basic (
ments of a program" at that time.[6]

Many personalities and events are recorded that influenced ea
program development, but one event in particular between two k
personalities is of special significance. That is a meeting betwe
Maurice DuPont Lee, chairman of E. I. DuPont de Nemours, a
William (Bill W.) Wilson, cofounder of Alcoholics Anonymo
(A.A.).[7] It is suspected that A.A.'s success in helping alcoholics sin
its beginnings in 1935 and Mr. Lee's need to deal with the proble
in the workplace were discussed, and perhaps the notion for an occ
pational program was fueled.

The first formal programs were implemented during this perio
but the industrial movement to drive drinking from the workplac
had actually begun before the turn of the century. *The Outlook*,
publication of that period, printed a ". . . succinct account of ho
sixty-three large firms in the Midwest had discovered that alcohol i
almost any quantities [sic] damaged efficiency." The firms' positio
on drinking in the workplace was that they ". . . used all manner o
ways, including discharge, to discourage the use of alcohol."

By the turn of the nineteenth century many other employers had
taken direct action on the serious drinking problem in the workplace.
The steel industry had begun dismissing employees for drinking on
the job and many American railroads required total abstinence—both
on and off the job.[8]

The Temperance Movement, Taylorism, and Workmen's Compensation were the motivating forces behind industries' efforts to rid
the workplace of alcohol. The moralistically desirable personal
characteristics of discipline, self-reliance, and hard work; the new
scientific concept of commercial efficiency; and the fact that the
employer would be held financially responsible for injuries incurred
by employees on the job were the major societal/industrial influences.[9]

In spite of these influences, alcohol and alcoholism were not
eliminated from the workplace. After a period of reduced consumption, drinking increased and efficiency became a serious concern,
once again, as we prepared for World War II. Three potent forces

panies with more than 5,000 employees offer EAP services.[16] The Association of Labor-Management Administrators and Consultants on Alcoholism (ALMACA) predicts that every employed person in the country will be covered by an employee assistance program by 1990.[17]

THE EVENTS THAT PAVED THE WAY

While this prediction may be somewhat exaggerated, the growth of employee assistance programming is evident. More and more employers are taking an active role in addressing drug- and alcohol-related problems in the workplace. A look at relevant events and activities since those early days of occupational alcoholism programming supports this fact:

1944 Dupont establishes the first known alcoholism program in a major multiplant company.

1944 National Council on Alcoholism (NCA) established.

1944 Eastman Kodak establishes the second major multiplant company program, handled through its medical department, with emphasis on Alcoholics Anonymous approach to recovery.

1947 International Doctors' group in A.A. established.

1956 American Medical Association recognizes alcoholism as a disease.

1959 NCA estimates that 50 companies have formal programs in full operation. The stereotype of the alcoholic person beyond help remains a deterrent to new program initiatives.

1960 NCA Industrial Committee established (later called Labor-Management Committee).

1965 NCA study indicates programs should place focus on job performance for the purpose of early identification of alcoholic employees.

1969 NCA's Labor-Management Committee established.

1970 Enactment of the Hughes Act establishes NIAAA-funded state programs.

1971 United Auto Workers International Executive Board adopts policy statement for joint union-management alcohol programs.

1971 Association of Labor-Management Administrators and Consultants on Alcoholism (ALMACA) formed.

1972 First Federal Aviation Administration exemption for alcoholism granted to air transport pilots.

1972 NIAAA offers staffing grants to support the work of two Occupational Program Consultants (OPCs) in each state.

1973 Approximately 500 occupational alcoholism programs in operation nationwide.

1974 Seventy-five percent of Blue Cross plans (62 percent of Blue Shield) have some degree of alcoholism coverage available.

1974 Air Line Pilots Association Human Intervention and Motivation Study (HIMS) begins operation.

1975 International Lawyers in A.A. group established.

1976 University of Missouri established employee assistance program for facility and staff.

1977 2,400 employee alcoholism programs are at some stage of development in public and private employment centers in all 50 states.[18]

And more recently:

1980 Baseball major leagues implement employee assistance programs.

1982 National Football League (NFL) enters into agreement with the Hazelden Foundation to provide EAP services for chemical-dependent players.[19]

1983 Several states pass legislation mandating insurance companies to offer coverage for alcoholism/drug abuse treatment.

1984 National Basketball Association (NBA) enters into contract with Control Data Corporation's Life Extension Institute to provide EAP for chemical-dependent players.[20]

1984 8,000 employee assistance programs addressing alcohol, drug, and other troubled employee problems are in place and operating.[21]

1985 ALMACA hires credentialing specialist in first step of process to build data base and develop criteria for credentialing EAPs.[22]

1986 Rockefeller College, State University of New York of Albany, plans to develop curriculum offering graduate degrees and/or certificates in employee assistance programming.

THE CHANGES AND THE CHALLENGES

Most organizations invest in employee assistance programs because the investment will yield returns in one form or another. These returns may be expressed in both quantitative and nonquantitative terms, a subject to be discussed fully in later chapters. It would suffice to say here, therefore, that most organizations with EAPs in place can show that such programs reduce both the cost of alcohol- and drug-related problems and the human suffering associated with such problems. When one considers the successful recovery rate of employees referred to EAPs—some organizations claim as high as of 75 percent—the value of the EAP is evident. Many employees who probably would have eventually lost their jobs, their families, and perhaps their lives are provided an opportunity to seek treatment and become productive employees once again.

The benefits of the corporate EAP are actually a synthesis of both economic and human returns. Like any company project with a focus on helping people, it benefits the population it serves by its very existence. Since the population it benefits is within the organization, it follows that the organization ultimately benefits.[23]

The challenge for organizations and for employee assistance programs does not lie, however, in the success they already know. The growth of the EAP movement since those first programs were implemented in the 1940s is evidence that the concept has been successful. This success and the value of having an EAP are not likely to change. The primary challenge lies in the changing employee population. While alcohol will continue to be America's number one problem, the troubled employee of the eighties is more likely to abuse many different drugs, including alcohol. Unlike the troubled employee of the recent past, this person will probably be chemical-dependent rather than a person who drinks too much. The values of this individual will also be different—sometimes only slightly, but different. "He" is as likely to be a "she." Words like "line," "free-base," "gram," "joint," and "straight" will be heard as often as "booze," "drunk," "martini," and "sober." Even the drinking habits in America are changing. "Bourbon and soda" and "scotch and water" are being replaced by more fashionable concoctions such as "Alabama slammer" and "sea breeze." The familiar neon silhouette of the martini glass has become a symbol of the changing times, sought after by collectors who know the value of that which once was. The challenge for the

EAP is not in identifying the "shot and beer" drinker or the heroin user, but in reaching the chemical-dependent employee and developing resources that will meet the needs of both employee and EAP. Organizations without EAPs in place can no longer ignore the growing problem of drugs in the workplace while existing EAPs must continue to modify their programs to remain effective.

Since many of the chemical-dependent persons will be using illegal drugs, there are legal questions that must be addressed. The employer who screens for drugs by taking blood or urine samples might present legal problems for the organization and/or the EAP. Ethical dilemmas are beginning to appear; for example, can the employer use a positive urinalysis to motivate the chemical-dependent person into treatment and then use a second positive urinalysis to fire that person? When does the treatment tool become a hatchet?

One of today's most pressing concerns is the question of compliance with federal and state antidiscrimination and confidentiality laws and regulations. Employers often assume that these laws do not apply to them; that only outside treatment programs must concern themselves with such issues. Suffice to say here that most EAPs are treatment programs and therefore must comply with federal and/or state regulations protecting the chemical-dependent person, a subject to be discussed further in later chapters.

An important consideration for both those organizations that have EAPs and those that do not is the growing concern of skyrocketing health-care costs. Alcoholism and drug abuse if left untreated will inevitably result in illness and injury requiring hospitalization. The cost of such hospitalizations is ultimately paid for by the organization through high insurance rates and disability claims. It is a cost that the organization without an EAP will have no control over. Many organizations with programs, however, are in a better position to monitor such costs. First, they will identify the chemical-dependent person at an early stage before the problem causes serious medical problems requiring hospitalization. Second, employees seeking treatment specifically for alcoholism or drug abuse would have to come through the EAP before being admitted to a hospital. Precertification before admission is especially effective when an incentive approach is used, that is, offering 90 percent coverage when EAP is used and only 50 percent if it is not.

Another important consideration is offering the services of the EAP to retired employees. Alcoholism is an increasing problem among the elderly and the risk of serious related health problems is even greater in this group. Most retirees are covered by the insurance policy of their last employer and the cost of treatment is paid through higher premiums. Where the organization is self-insured, this cost is even more evident. The availability of an EAP for this group is likely to reduce this cost, and equally important, provide a familiar and friendly resource for the retiree.[24]

The corporate response to alcohol- and drug-related problems in the workplace is twofold: first, a well-articulated policy and procedure that includes disciplinary procedures to be followed for rulebook violations and second, an employee assistance program prepared to provide quality service for those employees whose lives and jobs are affected by personal problems. An EAP is most effective in an organization where both the employer and the employee know where they stand.

NOTES

1. Howard V. Schmitz, *The Handbook of Employee Counseling Programs* (New York: The New York Business Group on Health, 1982), p. 15.

2. Ibid., pp. 26–31.

3. William S. Duncan, *The EAP Manual* (New York: National Council on Alcoholism), p. 20.

4. "Employee Assistance Programs: Training Needs and Resources," July 1984, p. 1. (Mimeographed.)

5. *Target: Alcohol Abuse in the Hard-To-Reach Work Force* (Rockville, Md.: National Institute on Alcohol Abuse and Alcoholism, 1982), p. 3.

6. Harrison M. Trice and Mona Schonbrunn, "A History of Job-Based Alcoholism Programs: 1900-1955," *Journal of Drug Issues*, ILR Reprint, Cornell University (Spring 1981): 178.

7. Walter Scanlon, "Trends in EAPs: Then and Now," *EAP Digest* 3 (May/ June 1983): 38–41.

8. Trice and Schonbrunn, "A History," p. 174.

9. Ibid., p. 173.

10. Ibid., p. 175.

11. *Target*, p. 2.

12. Trice and Schonbrunn, "A History," p. 176.

13. *Target*, p. 6.

14. Betty Ready, "ALMACA's Membership Problem," *The Almacan* 14 (April 1984): 3.

15. Duncan, *EAP Manual*, p. 11.

16. Chris Lee, "Is The American Work Force Stoned?" *Training* 20 (November 1983): 8–10.

17. Ready, "ALMACA's Membership Problem," p. 4.

18. *Target*, pp. 2–16.

19. James O'Hare, "EAPs in Professional Sports," *The Alamacan* 14 (May 1984): 3.

20. Ibid.

21. Reddy"ALMACA's Membership Problem," p. 3.

22. *The Almacan* 15 (January 1985): 1.

23. Scanlon, "Trends in EAPs," pp. 38–41.

24. Interview with Hank Linden of Brownlee, Dolan and Stein, New York, June 10, 1985.

4

EAP Practice and Process

GETTING THE EMPLOYEE THERE

There are at least three ways in which an employee can get to the company EAP: as a self-referral, as a medical referral, or as a supervisory referral. While some EAPs boast a self-referral rate as high as 60 percent, in most organizations employees are referred, directly or indirectly, by supervisors.[1] Even many employees who appear to be self-referred may actually have been prompted to contact the EAP during an informal supervisory confrontation.[2] Nevertheless, some employees do seek out the company employee assistance program on their own and avail themselves of the services offered, a subject fully discussed in Chapter 5.

In terms of the treatment offered to a self-referred employee versus that offered a supervisor-referred employee, there is, of course, no difference. Each will, hopefully, receive the same level of service. The difference is in what happens when the employee refuses to cooperate in treatment or decides to discontinue treatment. If the employee is self-referred, nothing happens. It was the employee who initiated the contact and it is the employee's right to discontinue treatment at will. The program counselor will usually make some effort to re-engage the employee if continued treatment is necessary, but the decision to continue remains the employee's.

An employee referred by the company's medical department may also have the right to refuse treatment if he or she chooses. Unless the employee's condition is affecting job performance, or the employee's behavior jeopardizes personal safety or the safety of others, a medical referral is not likely to be considered a condition of continued employment. The employee reserves the right to accept or refuse help. In this way a medical referral is similar to a self-referral.

The employee who is referred to the EAP by a supervisor, however, has a somewhat different status. The referral may have been made as an alternative to disciplinary action after a warning interview. While this employee also has the right of choice, refusing to accept the referral or not cooperating in treatment may trigger action leading to disciplinary procedures (see Figure 4.1). The warning interview, as used in many work organizations, is a specific management procedure applied when the employee's performance remains unsatisfactory following an earlier intervention interview. This happens regardless of whether or not the employee is currently engaged with the EAP. The warning interview initiates a probationary period during which the employee must achieve a satisfactory level of performance or face the possibility of a discharge.[3]

A term used to describe the process by which an employee is encouraged to seek out the services of the company EAP is often referred to as a "constructive confrontation," a term coined by H. M. Trice. He says:

> The decline in job performance that accompanies problem drinking is used as a basis for constructively offering alternative courses of behavior. Such employees should also be given emotional support and practical assistance, designed to direct them toward rehabilitation. Constructive confrontation represents an application of a social learning paradigm that is currently coming into prominence in the field of behavioral sciences.[4]

If the troubled employee is a member of a labor union, a union representative will usually be present during a constructive confrontation. In some cases, in fact, the union representative may be a party to the confrontation process. This is not likely to happen where the EAP is a management program but rather where the EAP is a joint union-management effort, a subject discussed in Chapter 7.

FIGURE 4.1. Procedural Flow Chart

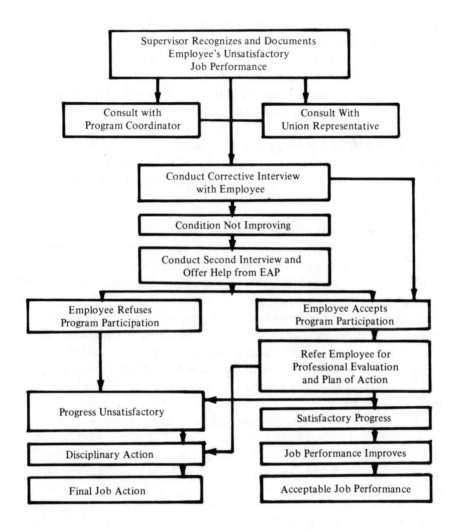

Source: Compiled by author.

THE SUPERVISOR'S ROLE

Whether the EAP is a union program, a joint union-management program, or a management program, the critical factor to its success is the chemical-dependent person's employment. The decline in job performance that accompanies the problem is used, as stated above, ". . . as a basis for constructively offering alternative courses of behavior." The constructive confrontation can be effective, however, only if the supervisor is doing the job he or she is expected to do: supervise. Knowledge about alcoholism, drug abuse, and other personal problems, as stated earlier, is not nearly as important as knowledge of the accepted and proven methods for dealing with these problems. There are five generally accepted basic steps which must be taken by the supervisor. These are:

1. *Recognition* that a problem exists and that there is a pattern of deteriorating work performance. When presenting the problem to the employee, it is important to describe the performance problem as observed and not to diagnosis or evaluate the personal problem causing the performance problem.

2. *Documentation* and keeping an up-to-date file of the employee's work performance are important. Without it, an otherwise effective confrontation can turn into a case of "your word against mine." Also, the employee may actually be unaware that job performance is affected. Having proof helps the employee to comprehend the problem as it actually is.

3. *Action* is the progressive formal disciplinary procedure consisting of informal verbal warnings, corrective interviews, work suspensions, and/or termination. Whatever the work organization does in terms of discipline, the important thing is follow-through on established disciplinary procedures.

4. *Referral* is the action of getting the employee to the company EAP. This is done directly or through the organization's medical department. A brief description of the events and/or behavior leading to the referral should be documented and forwarded. The EAP counselor uses this as a tool in penetrating the employee's denial. A treatment plan is formulated by the counselor that might include continued counseling, referral to an outside agency, self-help groups,

and/or rehabilitation in a live-in treatment program for up to eight weeks.

5. *Reintegration* is particularly important if the employee had been placed in a live-in rehabilitation program. Returning to work can be an anxiety-provoking experience and is a crucial phase of the employee's recovery. This can be minimized if both supervisor and employee know what to expect.

THE UNION REPRESENTATIVE'S ROLE

Although the terms "job jeopardy," "constructive confrontation," and "documentation" are associated with management programs and the supervisory referral process, these intervention strategies are also used by shop stewards and union delegates. The union representative is in a key position to identify the chemical-dependent union member even before the problem seriously affects job performance. As both a peer and a person who is in a position of authority, the representative's unique role lends itself to an effective constructive confrontation strategy—with concern. This applies whether or not the union has a formal program, management has a program, or a joint union-management program is operating. The union representative usually becomes aware of the problem through observation in the work place, personal interaction with the individual, or feedback from union co-members. An alert representative can frequently intervene in the earliest stages of dependency and effect recovery before the problem seriously affects the individual's family and job performance.[5]

Deteriorating job performance is management's concern, but it is also labor's concern. Work performance is a contractual issue. Union representatives manage the contracts in their handling of labor-management problems, and also function as liaisons between labor and management. They are actively involved in the definition of the contract and facilitate employer-union relations. Early intervention, therefore, provides an opportunity for labor as well as for management. While only management has the right to terminate an employee for unacceptable work performance, the union can most often influence that decision.[6]

WORK-RELATED INCIDENTS VS.
SYMPTOMS OF DEPENDENCY

Documentation of the troubled employee's deteriorating job performance is critical to an effective intervention. Work-related incidents should be noted and behavior directly related to the employee's responsibilities is the only kind of information appropriate to the constructive confrontation. While there are many clinical symptoms that could manifest in the chemical-dependent person, only those symptoms of deteriorating job performance should be discussed when confronting the employee. This is important for at least two reasons: First, confronting behavior not directly related to job performance is irrelevant and might be considered discriminatory. The Federal Rehabilitation Act of 1973 protects the alcoholic and drug abuser from discrimination and using information other than job performance may be in violation of this act. Second, while the supervisor may be aware of other nonwork-related symptoms, the supervisor is not a clinician and should not attempt to diagnose the problem. Even when the supervisor is aware of the nature of the problem, it is better not to discuss it. The intervention is more likely to be a success if the supervisor sticks with what a supervisor knows best: job performance.

THE DOs AND THE DON'Ts

This is generally the approach to an effective confrontation as applied by most work organizations. In addition, there are some DOs and DON'Ts that the supervisor must keep in mind. The DOs are: let the employee know that work performance is the company's primary concern; be aware that the problem will usually get worse without professional help; emphasize confidentiality when making the referral; explain that accepting a referral to the EAP will not necessarily exclude the employee from disciplinary procedures; be specific as to what is expected from the employee in terms of job performance; be objective, fair, consistent, and decisive.

The DON'Ts are: diagnose—leave that job to the EAP; discuss personal problems; moralize—keep the confrontation to job performance; counsel or be misled by emotional pleas; cover up for a friend.

The supervisor's cooperation is essential to the success of the employee assistance program. Unless the supervisor knows how to conduct a constructive confrontation, prepare in advance so that it will be a success, and make a timely referral, the troubled employee will be deprived the opportunity to get help and return to normal functioning. If a lack of such supervisory skills is organizationwide, then the EAP will be a failure. In order to prevent this failure, supervisors must learn the techniques and the process. Rather than firing or transferring troubled employees to other departments to "get rid" of the problem, appropriate use of the EAP can reduce the chemical dependency throughout the organization. The importance of the supervisor's role is emphasized in an *Alcohol World* article:

> The emergence of Occupational Alcoholism Programs (OAPs) not only provides a new mechanism for responding to employees with drinking problems, but also brings a new set of roles and responsibilities to the work environment. While the employee is the client of concern, the primary responsibility for the success of OAPs rests on the shoulders of supervisors.[7]

PROGRAM'S SUCCESS REDUCES
SUPERVISOR'S AMBIVALENCE

The role of the supervisor applies, of course, whether the program is an EAP or an OAP. The supervisor can be either a part of the problem or a part of the solution. If the problem is ignored, then there is no solution. This point is stressed because it is easier to ignore the problem than to deal with it appropriately. The supervisor may be competent and run a "tight ship" in every way, yet when personal problems are the cause of an employee's deteriorating job performance, all systems break down. The supervisor may feel that the problem is none of his or her business and that getting involved would be meddling. But job performance *is* the supervisor's business and getting involved where performance is deteriorating is the supervisor's job.

Reluctance to deal with deteriorating job performance that might be related to personal problems is not uncommon. The supervisor may sympathize with the troubled employee, or identify with the employee's problems, or be under the misconception that drinking is a solution to this employee's problems rather than the cause. Sometimes the supervisor's own drinking behavior, while not problematic, is an obstacle; that is, "How can I confront this employee when I probably drink more?" This is where the supervisor's understanding of the procedures for identifying and referring the employee are important: that it is not the drinking or drug use being confronted but rather the employee's poor job performance.

During a recent discussion I had with supervisors who had been promoted out of the rank and file, several admitted that they had some difficulty in confronting and referring employees to the organization's EAP. Even though they knew the referral would be based strictly on deteriorating job performance, their addressing the problem was made more difficult by the fact that they knew what the real problem was. This was particularly true where alcohol was the culprit. A few of the supervisors drank themselves, very often with the employees they supervised, and felt they could not confront the employee without encroaching on the individual's personal life.

The supervisor is often not that far removed socially from the person supervised, and a confrontation may be perceived as the end of a friendship. A constructive confrontation may actually be, in fact, the beginning of a relationship built on professional concern rather than on cover-up. The following is an example of one such case.

A unit manager recently told me that one of her administrative assistants had been promoted to the position of assistant manager. I knew the woman who received the promotion because she had been referred by the manager to our EAP 22 months earlier. The EAP counselor assessed the case at that time and referred her to a rehabilitation program for 28 days. She was a multi-substance abuser whose job performance showed a consistent pattern of deterioration. After completing the 28-day rehab program, she enrolled in a follow-up out-patient program that included group therapy, family counseling, and involvement in self-help groups. The employee responded very well to the EAP's treatment plan, obviously demonstrating her ability to recover and return, once again, to full productivity.

That's a short story with a happy ending. There is another story, however, within that story. The unit manager who had conducted the constructive confrontation with this troubled employee expressed her ambivalence to me at that time. She perceived the employee to be "shy and troubled" and feared that "reprimanding" her poor job performance at this time would make matters worse. The employee, nevertheless, was not getting her job done. The manager overcame her ambivalence, however, with one training session. After learning the strategies and techniques involved, she conducted an effective constructive confrontation and executed a successful referral to the EAP.

While it did not take long for the manager to realize the success of her intervention, this success was reinforced by a verbal expression of gratitude from the employee. Fourteen months after the constructive confrontation and referral to the EAP took place, the employee went back to the unit manager and said: ". . . I was very angry at the time. I felt I had been betrayed and could no longer depend on you to cover-up my problem. I was aware of the medical department's employee assistance program and knew that's where I'd be referred. I also knew, however, that I'd be able to manipulate the EAP and was planning my strategy even as you were confronting each incident of poor job performance. Boy, was I wrong—on both scores. The EAP had a 'plan' for me that made me look like an amateur manipulator. As for your taking the action that you did, all I can say is 'thank you.' That was the turning point of my life."

These remarks capture the essence of how most troubled employees feel after being referred to the EAP. The clinical and/or assessment skills of the EAP counselor in combination with the leverage that "job jeopardy" provides make the employee an excellent candidate for rehabilitation. The troubled employee is also a troubled person whose problem extends far beyond the workplace, and is often relieved, in fact, that finally it must be dealt with. This is an opportunity—the employee realizes in retrospect, of course—to lift a burden that probably would have been troubling the employee for years. Without the combined efforts of the supervisor and the EAP counselor this opportunity may never have presented itself.

JOB JEOPARDY IS AN EAP TOOL

This approach to dealing with alcohol- and drug-related job performance problems is sometimes referred to as the "job jeopardy" model. To be totally effective, "job discipline" and "constructive confrontation" procedures should be an integral function of the program.[8] This approach imposes penalties that ultimately lead to termination if the chemical-dependent employee refuses, discontinues, or does not respond to the EAP's efforts, and fails to maintain a satisfactory job-performance level.

Since one of the first signs of chemical dependency is a pattern of deteriorating job performance, the place of employment is a logical place to address the problem. Early recognition and intervention usually result in a more promising prognosis and successful rehabilitation. If a chemical-dependent employee is permitted to deteriorate without any serious steps being taken to confront and resolve the problem, then so too will work performance deteriorate. It is necessary for the supervisor to be thoroughly trained in recognizing patterns of declining job performance, maintaining documentation that supports these observations, and conducting a timely intervention and referral. A lack of supervisory training in program utilization undermines the program's potential effectiveness. In order for the supervisor to deal effectively with the problem of chemical dependence, the problem at hand—that of deteriorating job performance—must be dealt with expeditiously. Without adequate training, the supervisor may miss the problem or fail to refer the troubled employee to the EAP. In either case the program's effectiveness is diminished, the employee fails to get help, and the organization continues to pay the tab.

ATTITUDES AND PREJUDICES INHIBIT THE PROCESS

Stereotyping inhibits case finding in the workplace while misconceptions about the nature of the problem are barriers to employee assistance program development and/or program utilization. These misconceptions are reflected in the terms used to identify alcoholics and drug abusers. "There's nothing worse than a reformed drunk," for example, conjures the image of a self-righteous, proselytizing teetotaler, imposing his or her newly found sobriety in an uncompromising manner on anyone within earshot. This less than complimentary perception of the recovering alcoholic not only does nothing to remove the alcoholic's undeserved reputation as a weak-willed individual who cannot hold liquor, but also identifies an obnoxious person to be avoided even when sober.[9] Other expressions such as "He's on the wagon," or "She's off the sauce," suggest they will soon fall off the wagon and go back on the sauce. Derisive labels such as "pill-head," "junkie," "speed freak," and "cokehead" do little to further the notion that drug abusers are suffering from an illness.

While we are not likely to hear these expressions as often today, the underlying attitudes and misconceptions about the alcoholic and drug abuser are still held by many; and even though considerable progress has been made in educating the public to the fact that alcoholism is a treatable illness and that drug abuse is a medical problem, these concepts have not been embraced by all. In a recently produced documentary film about chemical-dependent women, several randomly selected pedestrians were asked how they felt about alcoholics and drug abusers.[10] The responses, for the most part, reflected their skepticism about the disease concept and the chance of recovery. Many expressed the opinion that sobriety was a matter of self-control and others had little faith in the recovery of drug abusers. When asked what they thought about women who drank too much or used drugs, they were even less forgiving—sex, promiscuity, and shades of moral indecency were the attitudes that prevailed.

In a recent training session designed to help supervisors identify and refer troubled employees to the company EAP, I asked the participants to write down single words they associated with alcoholics and drug abusers. Their responses included: drunk, dope, booze, theft, weak, untrustworthy, undependable, bar, needle, dry, violence, heroin, and jail. Such words as "illness" and "recovery" never appeared and "disease" was listed only once.

The point here is that the prevailing attitudes of society are also the prevailing attitudes of business and industry. This is not to say that society should suddenly "like" the chemical-dependent person, or that existing perceptions and misconceptions should make way for new information presenting alcoholics and drug abusers as victims of maladies not unlike diabetes or high blood pressure. On the contrary, business and industry should continue to "dislike" the chemical-dependent person and view him and her as personal and financial liabilities. But it should also recognize that the chemical-dependent person, like the diabetic, has a disease that cannot be cured but can be arrested; and that rehabilitation may prove a good investment. This does not mean that the corporation should seek out and hire active alcoholics and drug abusers as part of their affirmative action program efforts, but rather that it should make an effort to reach those already employed whose job performance is deteriorating because of such problems. The chemical-dependent employee is a fact of corporate life that cannot be ignored or wished away.[11] The rewards of such an effort will come in the form of reduced productivity losses and whatever value can be placed on a human life.

PROBLEM DENIAL AFFECTS ALL CONCERNED

Reaching the chemical-dependent person is sometimes easier said than done. Denial of the problem is a major obstacle to obtaining help for the drug or alcohol abuser. Unlike the diabetic who is likely to agree to treatment once the disease is diagnosed, the chemical-dependent person clings to the notion that "control" is possible. Even those friends and relatives who are close to the individual frequently deny the problem. A typical refrain might be, "Mary's not an alcoholic but she does drink too much sometimes." Using a variety of excuses and rationales, the chemical-dependent person will attempt to convince all concerned that the matter is under control.[12] Retorts such as "I don't drink any more than my friends do," or "I can part company with cocaine any time I choose to," or "Valium helps me get through the day" are not uncommon. There may, in fact, be an element of truth in these excuses. Many alcoholics do not drink much, and some drug abusers can stop for days at a time, and prescription drug misusers are not always aware of the seriousness of their problem. The problem, nevertheless, is evident in how it affects the individual's social/family relationships, health, or job performance.

Not only does denial of the problem make it difficult for the "helper" to offer help, but the fact that the chemical-dependent person becomes very skilled in convincing others that the problem really does not exist compounds it. This leaves the "helper," whether family member, friend, or supervisor, feeling frustrated and helpless— emotions not conducive to continued efforts to offer assistance. All concerned tend to ignore the problem, hoping it will go away. They seldom have enough information early in the progression of the illness and when it is finally out of control, the tendency is to cover up rather than confront. One reason for this is that once the problem is out in the open, someone has to find a solution. That responsibility usually falls upon whoever first abandons the notion that it might go away and admits, "We have a problem that must be confronted."

These dynamics apply both in the home and in the workplace. Many alcoholics have drunk themselves to death while friends, co-workers, family members, and supervisors hoped the problem might one day disappear. It is seldom a lack of concern that permits this to happen, but rather a lack of ability to turn concern into constructive action. In the workplace this ability comes in the form of a two-hour training program on identifying and referring the troubled employee to the EAP. It is here that the supervisor learns to store away whatever he or she knows about the employee's drug use, alcohol use, or personal problems, and applies the formula that has proven most effective in getting troubled employees back to full productivity once again: observation, documentation, confrontation, and referral. The supervisor's denial is removed once the training is conducted and the employee's denial is penetrated once the intervention takes place.

THE ROLE AND FUNCTION OF THE EAP COUNSELOR

The EAP counselor is the person responsible for seeing to it that the troubled employee receives the help necessary to correct the problem. This person may be a certified social worker, a credentialed alcoholism/drug abuse counselor, a psychologist, an M.A. in counseling, a psychiatrist, a nurse trained in counseling, or a person holding credentials in any combination of these disciplines. The EAP may employ a full complement of professionals from various disciplines, that is, psychiatry, psychology, social work, and counseling, or have only one person who assesses the problem and refers the employee to the appropriate outside resources(s) for assistance. The EAP counselor, whatever his or her professional credentials, is ultimately responsible for the troubled employee's treatment planning and/or knowing what treatment approach might be best applied.

Although some EAPs are prepared to provide a wide range of in-house services for the chemical-dependent employee, including a medical examination, ambulatory detoxification, counseling, and psychotherapy, most EAPs are not. Assessment, referral, and follow-up counseling are more typical. The counselor is responsible for coordinating treatment efforts, monitoring job performance through contact with the supervisor, and providing ongoing motivational and supportive counseling. This person must be qualified to identify and provide those services necessary to achieve success. Beyer and Trice define them as follows:

1. To overcome the employee's denial of the problem;
2. To motivate a change in behavior;
3. To get the employee into appropriate treatment, when needed;
4. To facilitate re-entry into normal roles after treatment;
5. To provide social supports to facilitate efforts to change behavior;
6. To monitor progress of the employee's change efforts and establish two-way feedback on results.[13]

These are the clinical functions of the EAP counselor that are critical to good treatment outcomes. The counselor must know what techniques will best penetrate the employee's resistance and then turn that resistance into motivation. A knowledge of treatment resources and when to use them is essential to both counselor and program success. It is important, for example, that the counselor does not overuse in-patient rehabilitation programs. A 28-day rehab experience can be a very powerful treatment tool, but its therapeutic benefits are limited. Its value, to a great extent, is in the learning experience it provides. This value diminishes with overuse, however, and the experience could instead become an "escape" from the job and from life's challenges.

Facilitating the employee's re-entry is a very important function that is frequently overlooked. It involves the supervisor, the employee, and the counselor. The employee must be counseled to facilitate the return to work after being away from the job for any length of time. If not handled skillfully, this could become a traumatic experience for the recovering alcoholic or drug abuser. The employee is extremely vulnerable at this point—afraid of rejection, questions, and of not being able to say "no." The supervisor needs guidance in handling the situation appropriately so as not to undermine the progress already made.

Providing social supports and monitoring the employee's progress are ongoing tasks for the counselor. Long-term treatment skills are important here if the counselor is assuming the role of primary therapist. If this function is left to an outside service provider, then the skill lies in knowing where motivational counseling ends and therapy begins. Under the best of circumstances, the counselor's role is ambiguous. A study on the subject of program functions indicated that the actual responsibilities of the counselor are so broad that "broker" is the best description. The study concludes:

> The core knowledge areas encompass alcohol/drug issues as well as emotional and relationship issues. Beyond these the EAP counselor may need some knowledge in the legal, financial or medical fields. Perhaps the two most needed skills in EAP counselors are ability to relate to a wide variety of people and ability to do quick, reasonably nonthreatening assessments. If an EAP program provides counseling in-house, then counselors need to be good counselors as well as good assessors.[14]

The EAP counselor is a professional and, like any professional, must know his or her limitations. This includes recognizing a problem that the counselor cannot solve, and knowing where to look for help. The counselor should be capable of identifying behavior that does not fit the profile of a chemical-dependent person, and knowing what resources will pick up where the EAP leaves off. When there is any question as to what the employee's problem may be, the employee must be referred to a resource capable of making that determination. In this sense, "broker" is an excellent description of an EAP counselor.

NOTES

1. "How Two Companies Curb Drug Abuse," *Occupational Hazards* 45 (April 1983): 95.

2. Discussion with Harrison M. Trice, New York State School of Industrial and Labor Relations, Cornell University, Ithaca, New York, August 1983.

3. "Alcohol & Drug Abuse Program Manual" (New York: Mobil Oil Corporation, 1978), p. 1. Offset.

4. Harrison M. Trice and Janice M. Beyer, "Social Control in Work-Settings: Using the Constructive Confrontation Strategy with Problem-Drinking Employees," *Journal of Drug Issues* ILR Reprint, Cornell University (Spring 1982); 21.

5. Madeleine L. Tramm, "Union-Based Programs," in *The Human Resources Management Handbook/Principles and Practice of Employee Assistance Programs*, ed. Samuel H. Klarreich, James L. Francek, and C. Eugene Moore (New York: Praeger, 1985), p. 97.

6. Ibid.

7. Norma R. Kurta, Bradley Googins, and Carol N. Williams, "Supervisors' Views of an Occupational Alcoholism Program," *Alcohol Health and Research World*, vol. 4, no. 3 (Spring 1980): 44.

8. Harold V. Schmitz, *The Handbook of Employee Counseling Programs* (New York: New York Business Group on Health, 1982), p. 27.

9. Alcoholism, like diabetes, has no cure; that is, "I *am* a diabetic," and "I *am* an alcoholic." The term "recovering" rather than "recovered," therefore, is preferred to describe an alcoholic who no longer drinks nor uses mood-altering chemicals. This applies no matter how long the person is alcohol and drug free.

10. Bonnie Friedman, "The Last to Know" (New Jersey: New Day Films, 1980).

11. Interview with Evan Mason, Mediplex Group, Inc., New York, June 3, 1985.

12. Harry Milt, *The Revised Basic Handbook on Alcoholism* (Maplewood, N.J.: Scientific Aids, 1977), p. 22.

13. Janice M. Beyer and Harrison M. Trice, "Design and Implementation of Job-Based Alcoholism Programs: Constructive Confrontation Strategies and How They Work," in *NIAAA Research Monograph No. 8/Occupational Alcoholism: A Review of Research Issues* (Washington, D.C.: U.S. Government Printing Office, 1982), pp. 181, 182.

14. Judy M. Winkelpleck, "Directions EAPs Move," *EAP Digest* 4 (July/August 1984): 19.

5

Marketing the EAP: Employees Who Refer Themselves

THE EAP AS AN EMPLOYER-SPONSORED BENEFIT

Many organizations describe their EAP as an employer-sponsored benefit designed to offer employees and family members assistance with personal problems. In addition to helping employees whose alcohol and/or drug abuse is interfering with their ability to function on the job, the EAP may assess, refer, and counsel employees who are experiencing problems at home, having difficulty in relationships, needing social services, managing finances poorly, gambling heavily, needing legal advice, or simply in need of someone to talk with. Depending upon the design and scope of the EAP function, the program may either provide services in-house or refer to appropriate community resources for assistance and/or treatment.

In organizations with comprehensive EAPs capable of handling a variety of personal problems, the self-referral rate is likely to be considerably higher than those programs focusing only on chemical dependency. This is because employees needing help with other problems are more likely to voluntarily seek out the services of an EAP than those who are experiencing alcohol- and/or drug-related problems. There are several factors that contribute to this phenomenon. The first is that denial of the problem is characteristic in drug and alcohol abusers, the abuser consciously and/or unconsciously not associating the substance with the emerging problems. Chemical dependency, therefore, is likely to progress to the point where other serious problems such as deteriorating job performance are evident. It is hoped that by this time the supervisor will have already referred the employee to the EAP. Second, rather than seeing alcohol and/or drug abuse as a problem, the troubled employee sees it as a solution to the problem. Voluntarily seeking help from the EAP would mean placing this "solution" in jeopardy. The third factor is that most other personal problems typically found in the workplace are of a short-term nature; consequently, the supervisor will not have observed deteriorating job performance over a long period of time.[1] While there are exceptions to this observation, these employees will discover the EAP or seek outside help before a supervisory referral becomes necessary.

TRUST AND CONFIDENTIALITY

In discussing employee assistance programming and supervisory referrals, the word "confidentiality" is usually used in the legal sense. It is likely to be followed by other legal terms and phrases such as "release of information," "code of federal regulations," "patient rights," etc. The alcoholic and drug abusing patient is protected under federal laws and state laws, and other troubled employees are protected under provisions of federal privacy acts and local laws where applicable. These laws, statutes, regulations, and guidelines are intended to protect all patients including employees using the services of the company EAP. Employees who are referred by supervisors as well as those who refer themselves are equally protected. Confidentiality, therefore, is assured whatever the employee's status may be. "Confidential communication," as described by the *American College Dictionary*, is "a confidential statement made to a lawyer, doctor, or priest, or to one's husband or wife, privileged against disclosure. . . ." "Trust," however, is "the obligation or responsibility imposed on one in whom confidence or authority is placed." The point here is that "confidentiality" is mandated by law while "trust" is assigned by a person.

The person who voluntarily seeks help from an EAP, albeit confidentiality is guaranteed, must also be assured that the person from whom help is being sought can be trusted. This means competence as well as confidence, and an unquestioning belief in the integrity, strength, and ability of the person entrusted. The employee who is likely to seek out an EAP for help, whatever the problem may be, either already knows or is hoping that the EAP professional can be trusted. The employee has either been assured by a fellow employee that the company EAP is reliable, or the EAP has successfully marketed its reliability and trustworthiness to the employee population. In either case the self-referred employee will approach the EAP professional somewhat cautiously, assessing the qualifications, credentials, and level of concern before making a personal investment.

In one of many cases following similar patterns, an employee telephoned my office and asked for information on alcoholism and what to do if a drinking problem seemed apparent. I talked with the employee for a short while and suggested a one-on-one counseling session to discuss the problem further, assuring the employee that confidentiality would be maintained. The caller rejected the offer, thanked me for the information, and promised to call again if necessary. The employee declined to leave a name.

Some weeks later I received a call, once again, from the anonymous caller. The caller had thought about what we had discussed previously and concluded that there did seem to be symptoms of an alcohol problem present. The caller admitted to having a safety-sensitive position, adding that while drinking on the job was not a problem, a reputation as a "drunk" might jeopardize job security. I responded, once again, to specific questions about alcohol abuse and treatment options available, adding that a personal meeting would better lend itself to discussing these options further. The employee reminded me that I mentioned "confidentiality" during our previous telephone talk and asked me specific questions about this aspect of the program. After a few more minutes of talking the caller thanked me for my time, this time asking if it would be all right to call in a few days. The caller, once again, declined to leave a name.

Two days later I received a third call from the same employee. This time the employee did not hesitate to give me a name, asked for an appointment to meet with me, and showed up promptly as scheduled. In our first meeting the employee continued to assess the program, exercising discretion and caution in both asking questions and providing answers. After the second session, however, the employee's uncertainty and caution had diminished and treatment planning became possible.

There is nothing dramatic about this case study. The point here, in fact, is to show the subtlety yet importance of establishing trust and emphasizing confidentiality. After the first telephone conversation the employee had enough information to choose any number of treatment options. These included several local treatment programs and self-help groups as alternatives to using the EAP directly. In talking with the employee and providing this information with no strings attached, the seed of trust had been planted. Through subsequent telephone talks and personal interviews the employee became satisfied that, whatever the organization's motives for providing such a service, the EAP practitioner showed both genuine concern and a pragmatic, professional approach to the employee's problem. This employee, incidentally, responded favorably to treatment and, at last count, had more than two years of continuous sobriety.

MARKETING TRUST AND COMPETENCE

Marketing is a human activity directed at satisfying needs and wants through exchange processes. *Exchange* is one of four ways in which a person can satisfy his or her needs. The other three are *self-production*, *coercion*, and *supplication*. The exchange process assumes four conditions, and while any one of these conditions may also apply to any one of the other three means to satisfying a need or want, none but exchange require all four:

1. There are two parties.
2. Each party has something that could be of value to the other.
3. Each party is capable of communication and delivery.
4. Each party is free to accept or reject the offer.[2]

If these conditions exist, then there is a potential for exchange. Whether or not the exchange actually takes place depends on whether or not the two parties can find terms of exchange.

In the process of marketing employee assistance, the employee population is one party and the EAP is the other. While marketing principles and philosophies of business organizations generally serve to "create" a need and, ultimately, actualize a potential exchange between seller and purchaser, these principles are also applicable where profit is not the bottom line. The marketing objectives for the EAP, however, are different. The objectives are closer to that of a nonbusiness organization or an organization engaging in social marketing. Marketing in the true sense is being responsive to the needs of the people.[3] In attempting to reach a market where the provider is not receiving direct payment for the services rendered, the success of the marketing efforts is often expressed in the number of people served. In this sense the marketing objective is truly "being responsive to the needs of the people," no strings (or cash) attached. Since the self-referred employee has not been referred by a supervisor, it could be assumed that job performance is acceptable; therefore, providing EAP services is truly a corporate act of altruism.

Whether or not this notion will "fly" under close scrutiny is not important. Even pure altruism yields rewards. What is important, however, is that the spirit of altruism is essential to reaching employees before deteriorating job performance becomes an issue. If the employee believes that there is a genuine interest in his or her well-being, then trust in the program has been established. If the EAP is staffed with professionals who know how to get their job done, then competence is also established. This does not mean that the EAP practitioner must be capable of treating every employee problem, or any at all for that matter, but resources must be available so that an appropriate assessment and/or referral can be made. If the EAP claims to help employees who are having financial problems, for example, or are seeking legal assistance, or are having drug problems, the program must deliver if it expects to project an image of trust and competence. "Delivery," as stated above, is one of the conditions of marketing.

Marketing the EAP is different from marketing a detergent or a soft drink. Unlike business marketing, the promoting of an EAP is closer to social marketing. It employs a change technology rather than a response technology, that is, getting people to stop doing something they want to continue to do. It is getting them to stop smoking, stop drinking, or stop using drugs.[4] While it can be argued that they *do* want to get help with their problems, this does not necessarily mean they want to give up whatever is causing their problems. A marketing strategy targeted to the person beginning to drink too much must provide the right message if a response is to be expected. A poster that states "We Help Alcoholics" is not, obviously, the right message.

Marketing an EAP is an integration of many separate functions: selling, distribution, advertising, research, development, and service. While training, not marketing, is important to the supervisory-referral process, a well-articulated marketing strategy is essential to building a program that will yield a high percentage of self-referrals. Trust and competence must be conveyed to the employee population, and while word of mouth will serve this objective to some extent, an ongoing marketing effort is necessary to satisfy all EAP marketing objectives. This marketing effort is best understood when it is divided into functions:

Selling focuses on the needs of the seller while marketing focuses on the needs of the buyer. It is, nevertheless, an important function in marketing the EAP. If the EAP administrator is convinced that the program is a quality service, then "selling" the program to the employee population becomes an important marketing function.

Distribution is that function of marketing critical to using the EAP services. Since the EAP is not a product that can be delivered to the employee's desk or work site, "distribution" means accessibility. The program location should not inhibit the chance of reaching any employee on any level. It should *never* be located in the personnel department. Ideally, the EAP should be in an insulated location where employees can feel safe, preferably away from the organization.

Advertising is the method(s) selected to provide the messages that project competence, trustworthiness, and availability (with no strings attached). Media selection is the problem of finding the best way to deliver this message to the target audience(s). Since every employee is a potential client, the target audience is the entire employee population. The employee population, however, is segmented into many subgroups: women, men, union, nonunion, management, clerical, black, white, etc. Groups are further divided by age, marital status, problem type, and so on. Advertising strategies should be designed to reach all segments of the population, such as: an article in the house organ about marital problems; a brochure targeted to the cocaine abuser; a presentation on all services available; a flier on help for employees with gambling problems; a film on women and drugs and how the EAP can help; a poster on helping the employee who may be experiencing a drinking problem; a white paper from the CEO restating the organization's policy on chemical dependency and/or other employee problems; or announcements of the EAP mailed directly to the home. The number of ways an EAP can advertise are limited only by the imagination of the program administrator. Whatever advertising vehicles are used, the message should always communicate that the EAP is a confidential service, and that confidentiality and trust will not be compromised under any circumstances!

Research is the function that allows the program to learn from its experience and shape the services to the employee's needs. Problem areas can be identified by reviewing where in the organization the self-referred employees are coming from, what kinds of problems they are coming with, how they learned about the program, what has happened since they came for help, how they were treated by the community program they were referred to, and any other information relevant to program development. This function also measures the effectiveness of advertising in terms of reach, frequency, and impact of the message delivered. The absence of self-referred employees from any particular department, division, or work site within the organization will alert the EAP administrator to a possible marketing problem.

Development follows research and can mean either developing new markets or developing new services. In learning about those "markets" within the organization that are not being reached by the EAP, marketing strategies could be developed to increase activity. The physical location of the EAP may not be good, or the language in the literature may be masculine and alienate women, or the brochures may be directed at front-line employees and missing management personnel, etc. Perhaps a woman, a minority person, a recovering alcoholic or drug abuser should be added to the EAP staff to attract hard-to-reach segments of the organization. The EAP may need to expand its services to reach a broader segment of the employee population, or it may have to market existing services more aggressively to encourage employees to use the program. Whatever action is taken, the objective of *development* is to reach those troubled employees that the EAP is potentially capable of reaching.

Service is the essence of employee assistance programming. In marketing language the EAP is called "a pure service" because there are no tangible goods exchanged.[5] Since the EAP's product is service, the service must be professional, accessible, and consistent. It is the EAP's responsibility to follow up on all employees who make contact to determine whether or not continued assistance is necessary. Marketing an EAP is like marketing a service warranty without the good. The EAP maintains credibility only as long as it is responsive to the needs of the employee population. It should never promise a service that it cannot deliver.

Marketing the EAP is a management function which needs the support of management to be effective. A strategic plan to reach the targeted employee populations is important, and tactical plans to facilitate program objectives are necessary, that is, literature, print media, education series, films. Most important, the marketing plan should include a realistic budget that reflects the tactical strategies in economic terms. This might include the cost of delivering quality services as well as the cost of making the EAP accessible to all employee levels.

While program awareness and program visibility are important in generating supervisory and union referrals, they are especially important in generating self-referrals. A program is not successfully implemented until it has been satisfactorily marketed within the organization.[6] And marketing to the troubled employee who has not yet exhibited related job-performance problems is an ongoing responsibility of the EAP. The chemical-dependent employee, as discussed above, will not seek out the EAP as frequently as other troubled employees might. But a planned marketing effort to target this population will certainly show positive results. An acronym that accurately reflects the process is "AIDA": Getting the employee's Attention; developing the employee's Interests; creating a Desire within the employee to resolve the problem; giving the employee an opportunity to take Action.

ARE SELF-REFERRALS REALLY SELF-REFERRALS?

Sometimes yes, sometimes no. A constructive confrontation conducted by a supervisor will often end on the note, "I suggest you get whatever help you need to bring your job performance up to par." Or the supervisor might recommend that the employee contact the company EAP. Or the employee may be under fire and make what he or she perceives to be a last-ditch effort to hold onto the job. While the EAP may carry this type of case as a self-referral, the factors motivating the employee are the same as those found in the supervisory referral model. The missing step is that the supervisor did not contact the EAP directly (or through the medical department) or did not require the employee to contact the EAP as a condition of continued employment. (Employees who are in safety-sensitive positions and are charged with drinking or using drugs while on duty are often required to accept treatment as a condition of continued employment.) The self-referred employee who has been told to "bring performance up to par" might be asked what precipitated the EAP contact, or whether or not there have been problems on the job. But in most cases supervisory pressure will be denied and a different picture will be presented than that which eventually emerges. Like the employee who is referred for counseling by the medical department because of a swollen liver, or the union member who is advised to seek help by the shop steward, this type of case might be classified as a "soft-referral" rather than a supervisory or self-referral. Progressive disciplinary procedures in some organizations require an "intervention interview" followed by a "warning interview" if job performance does not improve. This type of self-referral is often generated by the intervention interview.

A peer-referral might be viewed as either a soft-referral or a self-referral. While many organizations have EAPs with peer-referral rather than supervisory-referral designs, an informal peer-referral network can serve the same objective: to get help for the troubled employee at the earliest possible stage. "Camaraderie, mutual concern, and care are as much a part of the world of work," says Dan Molloy in a study on the peer-referral model, "as supervision, performance, and accountability. Both can work toward assisting the troubled worker."[7] The lines that separate the soft-referral from the self-referral from the supervisory-referral can be very thin. The notion of self-referral, nevertheless, allows the EAP to present itself as the employees' ally, and encourages employees to present themselves as responsible adults rather than people whose behavior is offensive and must be regulated.[8] The influences motivating the employee to seek help might be as obvious as poor job performance or as nebulous as not feeling good about one's self. Indeed, employees do not simply get up one morning and decide to go to the EAP; their decisions are made through socialization and interactions with other people.[9] Whatever influences precipitate the employee's decision to seek help, the EAP must present itself as a professional, confidential, and competent function of the organization to assure that employees who *might* refer themselves *do* refer themselves.

THE EAP AS A FLAGSHIP BENEFIT

The EAP is a direct benefit provided by the employer for the employee. Using the program requires no outlay of money by the employee and whatever the problem may be, it can often be resolved without treatment expenses. If it becomes necessary to refer the employee to a community resource, a search for the best possible alternative at the lowest possible cost is expected. Company insurance plans sometimes cover the entire expense.

The value and benefits of employee assistance programming will be discussed fully in Chapters 9 and 10. It will suffice to say here then that humanistic as well as economic benefits are expected and that extended benefits to the employee's family and community are important considerations. Public policy, social responsibility, and corporate social responsiveness have been noted as good reasons to help employees with their personal problems. All these benefits, values, and reasons for offering the services of an EAP apply regardless of the scope of the program or the path by which the employee gets there. The success of the EAP is often measured, in fact, by the supervisors' use of the program rather than the employees' use of the program. That is, the ratio of supervisors to supervisory-referrals is more significant than the ratio of total employees to total EAP cases. The significance is that it shows a regiment of supervisory personnel well trained and skilled in the process of identifying and referring troubled employees. Self-referred employees, however, lend credibility to the program as a service for *all* employees and not just for those who are in trouble. An employee experiencing the start of a drinking problem, for example, is likely to seek help from an EAP on the advice of a colleague who is successfully recovering through the program.

Equally important to the program's credibility are the favorable experiences of troubled employees who come to the EAP for advice on personal matters other than chemical dependency, or seek help for family members. When these types of problems are successfully resolved the employee appreciates the EAP as a true benefit and projects this attitude to fellow employees. A number of such successful outcomes in an organization will go far to promote the EAP as a valuable service that any employee might use.

Almost all organizations offer some form of indirect compensation, fringe benefits, or supplemental compensation. In some companies this may account for 50 percent of the total compensation package. In return, the organizations expect to fulfill several objectives that include:

- Attracting good employees
- Increasing employee morale
- Reducing turnover
- Increasing job satisfaction
- Motivating employees
- Enhancing the organization's image among employees
- Making better use of compensation dollars
- Keeping the union out[10]

The EAP is a form of indirect compensation and while not all of the above objectives are fulfilled in providing such services, some are. The existence of an EAP is not likely to be an incentive to a prospective employee, but for the incumbent employee the value of a program is in proportion to the services offered. The concomitant value to the organization can be quantified, in fact, where recovery of the chemical-dependent person increases productivity and reduces costs. The objectives listed above, however, are viewed more as an investment in human capital, that is, investing in employees in the same way the organization might capitalize a physical plant, machinery, or inventory.[11] When viewed in this way, the EAP becomes an investment in the future and, since any employee might use the services of the EAP at some point in time, its value becomes far greater than that measured through cost-benefit analyses alone. Reaching the employee who might voluntarily seek out the services of the EAP then becomes at least as important as developing an effective supervisory-referral model.

NOTES

1. Lewis F. Presnall, *Occupational Counseling and Referral Systems* (Salt Lake City: Utah Alcoholism Foundation, 1981), p. 187.

2. Philip Kotler, *Marketing Management*, 4th ed. (Englewood Cliffs, N.J.: Prentice-Hall, 1980), p. 19.

3. Robin E. MacStravic, *Marketing Health Care* (Germantown, Md.: Aspen Systems, 1977), p. 7.

4. Walter F. Scanlon, "Non-Business Marketing Becomes Required Strategy," *Fund Raising Management* 14 (August 1983): 48.

5. Kotler, *Marketing*, p. 374.

6. James L. Francek, "Marketing an EAP For Success," in *Human Resources Management Handbook/Principles and Practice of Employee Assistance Pro-*

grams, ed. Samuel H. Klarreich, James L. Francek, and C. Eugene Moore (New York: Praeger, 1985), p. 28.

7. Daniel, J. Molloy, "Peer Referral: A Programmatic and Administrative Review," in *Human Resources Management Handbook/Principles and Practice of Employee Assistance Programs*, ed. Samuel H. Klarreich, James L. Francek, and C. Eugene Moore (New York: Praeger, 1985), p. 108.

8. William J. Sonnenstuhl, "Understanding EAP Self-Referral: Toward a Social Network Approach," *Contemporary Drug Problems*, reprinted by Federal Legal Publications (1984), p. 288.

9. Ibid., p. 289.

10. Randall S. Schuler, *Personnel and Human Resource Management* (St. Paul, Minn.: West, 1981), pp. 308, 309.

11. Carl J. Schramm, "Evaluating Occupational Programs: Efficiency and Effectiveness," in *NIAAA Research Monograph-8/Occupational Alcoholism: A Review of Research Issues* (Washington, D.C.: U.S. Government Printing Office, 1982), p. 367.

6

The Standards,
the Structure,
the Climate

CREATING A BODY OF KNOWLEDGE

The growth of employee assistance programming has produced a body of knowledge important to both program planners and operators. Research and experience in the field are the bases for formulating the standards and guidelines that are the foundation of any effective program. While this book's focus is on those programs that are in-house, these standards apply to any form of EAP service. This includes consulting firms that contract with work organizations and/or labor unions, and organizations that join together in a consortium sharing a central EAP service.

These standards are also applicable to any size organization in any sector. Private corporations, large and small, labor unions, municipalities, law enforcement agencies, public organizations, professional groups and associations apply these guidelines in developing and operating their programs. Without the program structure that these standards provide, EAP management is likely to be by crises rather than by objectives.

These standards were formulated by the blue-ribbon Program Standards Committee, a group of leaders in the fields of employee assistance programming, personnel management, and labor relations. The committee was formed in a special meeting called by the National Council on Alcoholism (NCA) in which representatives from the federal government, from organized labor, and from the Association of Labor-Management Administrators and Consultants on Alcoholism (ALMACA) participated. Holding its first meeting in New York City on January 14, 1980, the committee took its initial step in developing the first complete set of standards for employee alcoholism and/or assistance programs. These standards are divided into five major categories: (1) policy and procedure, (2) administrative functions, (3) education and training, (4) resources, and (5) evaluation.[1] The following is an adaptation of these standards modified to include drug-related as well as alcohol-related problems in the workplace.

Policy and Procedure

There must be a written policy statement on alcoholism and drug abuse and on any other problems to be addressed by the EAP. This should be signed by the chief executive officer and, in joint labor-management programs, the union president. The policy should state that alcoholism and drug abuse are medical problems amenable to treatment and rehabilitation. The policy should also specify the respective responsibilities of management, union representatives, and employees as they relate to the program. The EAP need not in any way alter management's responsibility or authority or union prerogatives, and participation in the EAP should not affect future employment or career advancement; nor will participation protect the employee from disciplinary action for continued substandard job performance or rule infractions.

Confidentiality is an essential ingredient in any EAP. For this reason written rules are established to specify how records are to be maintained, for what length of time, who will have access to them, which information will be released to whom, and under what conditions, if any, can records be made available for the purposes of research, evaluation, and reports. Client records maintained by an EAP should never become part of an employee's personnel file. Adherence to federal regulations on confidentiality of alcohol and drug abuse records (42 CFR Part 2) is required of programs receiving federal funds, even indirectly.

This standard applies equally to employees who are referred by supervisors as well as employees who refer themselves. Regardless of how the employees get there, there is often a lingering concern about using the EAP. Typically, they want to be assured that it will not cost them any money, that they can go during work time, and that their confidentiality will be protected. The first two issues are resolved immediately, but questions about confidentiality linger long after the employee is referred to treatment and the presenting problems have been resolved.[2]

Procedures for referring employees are critical to a program's success. The EAP administrator should prepare a written procedure for action to be initiated by management and/or union representatives. This will provide for an assessment and evaluation by EAP professionals, referral to a community resource if necessary, feedback to and from the referral source, and a plan for follow-up and continued treatment, if necessary. The procedures should be a terse and exact plan of action that begins with documenting the troubled employee's deteriorating job performance and ends with the employee back on the job and functioning at an acceptable level. The procedures will also include, of course, whatever action is necessary when a troubled employee refuses to cooperate, or when job performance remains poor even after assistance is offered.

Procedures for voluntary use of the program by employees and/or family members are equally important. A high percentage of self-referrals lends credibility to the EAP. When employees seek out the EAP for assistance in personal matters, procedures will provide guidelines for assessment and evaluation by EAP professionals. They will also facilitate treatment planning including referrals to community providers and provisions for follow-up services. Consistent with confidentiality regulations, the program will initiate no contact with management concerning individuals who refer themselves, nor will it acknowledge the participation of any such employee.

The policies and procedures established by the organization should be known to all employees and supervisory personnel. Many organizations print brochures that introduce the company EAP, describe how it works, state who may use it, and discuss the policies that govern its use. The following is an example of such a policy:

- This organization is concerned with the effects of alcohol or drug abuse on the health of its employees, but believes it can legitimately intervene only when the individual's job performance becomes affected.
- Alcohol and drug abuse are health problems that are treatable. Employees suffering from these illnesses will be given the same

consideration and offer of assistance, under applicable employer benefit plans and programs as are presently extended to employees with other illnesses.

- The social stigma often associated with alcohol and drug abuse tends to discourage those who need help from seeking and accepting treatment. An enlightened attitude and realistic acceptance of these conditions as illnesses will encourage employees to take advantage of available confidential diagnostic counseling and treatment services when needed.

- An individual's employment will not be in jeopardy solely because the individual is suffering from an alcohol or drug problem so long as: (a) the employee seeks treatment, and rehabilitation proceeds satisfactorily as indicated by confidential communications between the treatment resources and the EAP, and/or (b) job performance is or becomes satisfactory.

- Confidentiality of records and communications on any employee under the care of the EAP will be maintained in the same manner as is maintained for other medical problems. Where alcoholism or drug abuse is the problem, these records must be maintained in adherence to federal regulations protecting these cases (42 CFR Part 2), or in accordance to any applicable municipal, state, or federal regulations or guidelines.

- Implementation of this policy will not require or result in any special regulations, privileges, or exemptions from standard personnel administration practices while the employee is on the job. Performance problems will be handled in accordance with established employee-employer procedures.

- This policy is not to be interpreted as constituting any waiver of management's responsibility to maintain discipline or its right to invoke disciplinary measures in the case of misconduct which may result from, or be associated with, the use of alcohol or drugs.

- The sale, distribution, or medically unauthorized use or possession of narcotics and other dangerous and/or illegal drugs by employees on this organization's premises is prohibited and shall be grounds for termination.

Administrative Functions

The organizational position of the EAP should be at the management level. Responsibility for the operation of the EAP should be positioned at a management level high enough to insure the involvement of senior management and/or union leadership in sustaining the program. The EAP professional must relate effectively to all levels of the organization and, to do this effectively, this person should be a ranking staff member.

The physical location of the EAP offices should facilitate easy access while insuring confidentiality. A program that is located in the middle of the personnel department, for example, is an implicit violation of the employee's right to confidentiality. It will preclude any sense of trust and also discourage self-referrals.

A carefully designed record-keeping system will protect the identity of the client while facilitating case management and follow-up. This system should allow for rapid and ready access to statistical information.

There should be a relation of the EAP services to medical practices and disability benefit plans. This should be reviewed periodically to insure that benefits adequately cover diagnosis and treatment for alcohol, drug, and mental health problems. Where feasible, the insurance plan should provide coverage for out-patient, in-patient, and day treatment care for both the troubled employee and family members. The EAP staff should be familiar with the provisions of the medical and disability benefit plans so they can advise clients clearly as to the extent, nature, and cost of the recommended treatment and reimbursement available.

Malpractice and liability insurance is an important investment for the EAP just as it is for any other medical program, and the organization should conduct a legal review of all aspects of the program. The purpose is, of course, to ensure that there is adequate protection for all EAP staff, and that the organization is protected against possible malpractice and/or liability claims.

The qualifications of the EAP staff should be established, and collectively they should combine two primary qualifications:

1. Administrative skills including managerial, marketing, and human resources experience and,

2. Clinical skills in interviewing and assessing problems, in motivational counseling, and in identifying appropriate treatment resources. Experience and expertise in dealing with alcohol- and drug-related problems are essential. (EAPs that do only assessment and referral do not necessarily need a full complement of administrative and clinical skills.)

Education and Training

The organization should be communicating the availability of EAP services to employees and their families. It is important that the employees and their families are informed about the organization's program and the availability of its services. This information must be updated whenever necessary and new employees should be advised upon hiring of the services available.

The organization should have a major commitment to educating its employees on problems inherent in the use and abuse of alcohol and drugs. Additional efforts should be made to provide employees with information that might help identify other problems of a personal nature. While this is a service to all employees, it will also serve to reduce the denial in those employees who are presently experiencing problems with alcohol and/or drugs. Constructive confrontation is more effective when the employee has some awareness of the disease concept of alcoholism and drug abuse.

A program orientation for both supervisors and union representatives is necessary for successful program utilization. The training objective is a working understanding of policy and procedure and an understanding of their respective roles in the process. This should be done on a periodic basis.

Resources

The EAP should maintain a resource file on outside providers of assistance. This file should contain current information about alcoholism treatment services and other resources. Information should include all self-help alcoholism and drug-abuse groups for the chemical-dependent persons and their families as well as a comprehensive listing of appropriate health care facilities, community services, and other professional service providers.

Evaluation

A periodic program review and evaluation is necessary to insure an objective critique of operations and performance. This process will provide feedback for program modification when necessary.

Staff performance evaluation is also necessary to insure that EAP staff are functioning optimally. Quality of care and program effectiveness are contingent upon a skilled and professional staff.

PROGRAM STRUCTURE AND FUNCTIONS

The employee assistance program can be divided into four components: administrative, educational, clinical, and research/evaluation. The functions of all four components may be carried out by one EAP staff member or many staff members, depending upon the scope of the program and the size of the organization. A program providing a wide range of services in addition to chemical dependency services would require a higher staff/employee ratio. An organization with work sites, corporate offices, and/or service facilities at various locations would also require a higher staff/employee ratio. This is particularly true if all services are provided in-house and not contracted to an external EAP service provider.

The administrative component of the EAP has personnel, marketing, and management functions. Knowing the channels of communication, personnel policies, and procedures that might impact on program objectives and treatment planning is important. A knowledge of employee benefits, disability plans, educational forums available to employees, medical department functions, legal constraints and employee rights is essential to good programming. The EAP may even serve to satisfy some Equal Employment Opportunity Commission (EEOC) regulations and Occupational Safety and Health Administration (OSHA) standards. An understanding of applicable federal and local laws on confidentiality and on legislation protecting the employee against discrimination is a priority.

An understanding of both business and health-care operations is important to whoever is charged with the administrative responsibilities of the EAP. This includes knowing how to deal with the chain of command and knowing how to get action within the organization. Managing and marketing the EAP effectively mean coordinating all of the program's functions to achieve maximum reach and provide quality services.

The educational component serves to orientate employees, supervisors, and management to the company EAP. It provides the general employee population with information on preventive health care and trains the supervisory staff on program utilization. As discussed earlier, identifying the chemical-dependent employee and making an appropriate referral to the EAP involve knowing the process and procedure. The EAP must be staffed to provide these educational services and serve as a consultant to management, supervisors, and employees. Formal and informal training sessions facilitate these objectives.

The importance of the clinical component of the EAP cannot be overstated. Where the education component is the "mind" of the EAP, the clinical component is the "heart." For the EAP to achieve optimum effectiveness, its diagnostic resource must be an integral part of the operation and should not be an independent outside unit.[3] While the other three components are essential to the EAP's effectiveness, the clinical component is essential to the EAP's existence. There can be no compromising here; the person responsible for assessing employee problems and developing plans of action must be a professional.

The research/evaluation component demonstrates the EAP's value in both quantitative and qualitative terms, quantitative in that it provides an absolute measure of program participation and qualitative in that it also measures degrees of success. Cost benefit, cost effectiveness, and program reach are determined, and impact on employee morale and attitude, to whatever extent possible, is measured.

CREATING A CLIMATE CONDUCIVE TO EAP UTILIZATION

There are several factors that will influence and encourage the use of the EAP and contribute to the success of its efforts. Program credibility and management support are probably the two most important. Program credibility, in fact, is not possible without management support. The success of the program depends to a great degree on how it is perceived by the organization, and the organization's perception is shaped by the importance management places on the EAP function:

The EAP should become an integral department of the corporation with the same opportunities for intracorporate communication as other departments. Only in this way can the EAP perceive the pulse of the corporation and help it deal more effectively with its human resources.[4]

Program credibility, therefore, starts with an endorsement from management through the formulation and distribution of a corporate policy statement. As discussed under policy and procedure above, this statement should reflect the organization's position on chemical dependency, affirming that alcoholism and drug abuse are serious health problems amenable to treatment. It should stress the importance of existing disciplinary procedures in program utilization, and should assure program participants that neither future employment nor career opportunities will be affected in any way. Confidentiality of all program records must, of course, be assured.

This is a start. A policy statement signed by the chief executive officer, and the union president if the program is a joint effort, is an essential first step in establishing program credibility with employees, supervisors, and union representatives. The troubled employee learns that chemical dependency is a health problem, the supervisor is introduced to the concept of "job jeopardy" as a tool to help the employee, and the union representative becomes aware that early intervention is the best strategy. The policy underscores the supervisor's role in getting the troubled employee to the EAP. A policy statement is a necessary prerequisite to an EAP's success, but it alone will not provide program credibility. Like a cornerstone in a building, it is the starting point from which the program is built.

From the troubled employee's point of view, action speaks louder than words. Confidentiality, job security, and the opportunity to get help must be demonstrated. Credibility is a growing process that comes as the employee population hears good things about the program. The employee must see the EAP as an employee service without a hidden agenda and the EAP counselor as a professional who can be trusted. The ethical standards established to guide the program must render it beyond reproach, and the integrity of the program must never be compromised.

From the point of view of the supervisor, "credibility" takes on a different meaning. The supervisor who refers a troubled employee expects the employee's job performance to improve. Where this is not happening, or where relapses occur, a dialogue between supervisor and program is important. This communication should never violate confidentiality requirements, but should serve to facilitate treatment and management objectives. As the supervisor begins to see program results, an appreciation of the EAP function develops. Through training and ongoing consultation with the EAP practitioner, the program's benefits are realized and the supervisor's skills in dealing with the chemical-dependent employee are sharpened.

Unless credibility is established with both employees and supervisors, the program's success will be limited. The EAP's objective is to return the employee to the workplace ready to do a day's work. This objective can be realized through strategic intervention—a function of the supervisor who has skillfully carried out those tasks essential to making an appropriate referral—and an EAP ready to provide assistance. Even the most resistant supervisors cannot argue with success. A high percentage of EAP referrals improve job performance and achieve lasting sobriety both on and off the job. The key to this success is simply using the job as a lever to get the employee to the EAP for assistance. As discussed in Chapter 4, the supervisor achieves this objective by applying those skills that are a function of being a supervisor: observation, documentation, and confrontation. Two more steps, referral (of the employee to the EAP) and reintegration (of the employee back to work), are added.

Creating a climate that will encourage program utilization is an administrative function. This includes effective program management, planned marketing strategies, and well-articulated policies and procedures congruent with existing personnel practices. In terms of effective program management and existing personnel practices, the supervisor must be able to communicate with the EAP in the same way that he or she communicates with any other work unit within the organization. The purpose of a staff function—and the EAP is a staff function—is to facilitate line management in getting the job done. The supervisor should not have to learn medical, social work, or counseling jargon, nor should a new set of policies be developed that "talk" a different language. The role and perception of the supervisor will influence the climate that ultimately determines program success. It is important, therefore, that program development include significant input from line supervisory personnel, and from union representatives if the organization is a union shop. It is a management function to take this input and develop a program that reflects the objectives of the organization.

The importance of a planned marketing strategy has been discussed in detail in Chapter 5. In marketing the EAP to reach those employees who might never be referred by a supervisor, the organization is creating a climate that will encourage both self-referrals *and* supervisory-referrals. Educating the general employee population about drugs and alcohol serves to raise consciousness and brings the subject of chemical dependency out into the open. While the marketing objective is to reach those employees who are experiencing problems, this objective is realized by creating an environment where such employees are not stigmatized. The marketing strategy should be thought of as an ongoing campaign to remove the stigma associated with chemical dependency, and to create a climate of openness and awareness. The awareness allows individuals to make intelligent choices about the use of mood-altering chemicals, while openness respects the choices that others make. But most important, a well-orchestrated, organizationwide education program will reduce drinking and drug use in the workplace and encourage the use of the EAP when such problems do exist. The Federal Railroad Administration, for example, launched a nationwide program in 1985 designed to reduce the use and abuse of alcohol and drugs on the job. The program, which is called "Operation Redblock," is being adopted by railroads throughout the country in an effort to change the railroad industry's image as a hard-drinking work culture. While the adoption of EAPs by railroads is an inherent goal of Operation Redblock, the emphasis is on alcohol and drug education.

An ongoing promotion campaign should be designed to create an environment where the use of alcohol and/or drugs is not acceptable behavior and provide information on where to turn for assistance if necessary. Print, posters, and bulletins are effective ways to reach the employee population. Articles should appear on a regular basis in the organization's newsletter, fliers can be enclosed with paychecks, and posters emphasizing "confidential help" should be strategically displayed. Many organizations make an effort to reach the employee's family by mailing announcements to the employee's home. Since the troubled employee is also a troubled family member, involving the family at this level can be important to early identification of the problem. This is especially important when the troubled employee is troubled not because of a personal chemical-dependency problem, but because a loved one at home is in trouble with alcohol or drugs. Reaching out to family members is a sure way to establish credibility with the employee population.

Program accessibility should be built into the program's design. Because the EAP provides a human service, the service should be available on any given day. Some organizations may not be large enough to justify a 24-hour program but use an answering service during nonbusiness hours. This is an inexpensive but very effective alternative. It is important, however, that calls from both troubled employees and supervisors be returned promptly, and appointments scheduled at the earliest possible convenience. Program credibility and program utilization are generated through prompt, professional service and visible results.

The EAP is most effective in a synchronous environment. Creating this environment is, to a great extent, the program's responsibility. Its procedures should be easy to understand and required paperwork should be kept at a minimum. Like any function or service of a work organization, the EAP must continuously evaluate its results and make appropriate changes in direction when necessary. The real value of an EAP is in its problem-solving ability. In order to continue to be of value, it must be ready to meet the needs of the employees as well as the needs of the managers and the supervisors expected to deal with the problems.

The standards by which the EAP operates and the climate that it operates in will determine its effectiveness in reducing alcohol and drug-related job-performance problems. While the EAP alone will not solve the problem of chemical dependency in the workplace, it is an important part of the solution. It is a pragmatic approach to a human problem that is designed to provide a solution for both employee and employer. The chemical-dependent employee is provided an opportunity to receive assistance and both employee and employer profit as a result.

NOTES

1. Blue Ribbon Program Standards Committee, comprised of representatives from the Association of Labor-Management Administrators and Consultants on

Alcoholism; the National Council on Alcoholism; the Occupational Program Consultants Association; the National Institute on Alcohol Abuse and Alcoholism; the U.S. Office of Personnel Management; and the AFL–CIO and other segments of organized labor, "Standards for Employee Alcoholism and/or Assistance Programs," (New York: January 1980).

2. William J. Sonnenstuhl, "Understanding EAP Self-Referral: Toward A Social Network Approach," *Contemporary Drug Problems* (1984): 269–93.

3. John Dolan, "The Staffing Requirements of Employee Assistance Programs," in *Mental Wellness Programs for Employees*, ed. Richard H. Egdahl and Diana Chapman Walsh (New York: Springer-Verlag, 1980), p. 131.

4. Ibid., p. 133.

7

Unions, Managements, and Joint Programs

LABOR UNIONS' DISTRUST OF MANAGEMENT EAPs

A management-operated employee assistance program is often viewed with suspicion by the bargaining unit. The unilateral formulation of a chemical-dependency policy and the implementation of an EAP might even be in violation of the collective bargaining agreement. Any action taken by the employer, in fact, that has not been negotiated at the bargaining table could be considered a violation of the terms and conditions of employment. Referring an employee to the company EAP for an evaluation, for example, might be grounds to file a grievance. At the very least, union members are not likely to voluntarily seek help from a management-operated program for problems related to alcohol and/or drug use or abuse. This is especially true if the employee is in a safety-sensitive position where the use of mood-altering chemicals could result in termination. Union representatives will seldom, if ever, refer a union member to a management EAP. The exception to this is where the EAP has earned the trust of the union over a long period of time and the program's credibility has been established.

While joint union-management programs have proven successful in helping both the chemical-dependent employee and eliminating time-consuming, no-win grievance procedures, EAPs without union input do not enjoy the same level of cooperation. The EAP, in fact, is frequently seen as a device of the personnel department for the purpose of reducing costs and/or complying with progressive disciplinary action procedures. This is true even when the program is a function of the organization's medical department. Consequently, the management EAP is likely to be used by unions only as a last resort to circumvent disciplinary action against union members. This is not to say that all management programs are tabooed by union members, but establishing any level of trust may take years to achieve.

The union is, of course, right in part. While no ethical EAP would ever allow itself to be used against any employee, most EAPs are a function of management with an objective to reduce the costs of alcohol- and drug-related problems in the workplace. The union can appreciate management's objective, even though it views the problem from a different perspective. It sees the chemical-dependent employee as a brother or sister in trouble or as a human problem that requires intervention rather than as a cost problem that must be contained. Union representatives talk of helping those suffering from alcoholism and drug abuse while management executives talk of reducing the cost of chemical dependency in the workplace. One such union officer with the International Association of Machinists and Aerospace Workers union says:

> I believe that this most dreaded disease, alcoholism, can be overcome with the helpful compassion and understanding of our fellow brother and sister human beings.[1]

From a management point of view, however, the focus is cost containment. A staff person from National Car Rental says:

> I can't even estimate what drug use has cost this company. I think it's the biggest problem in industry today. Nothing else is even in second place compared to it.[2]

The union executive speaks of "compassion and understanding" and the corporate executive talks of company "cost." While joint union-management programs transcend these differences in the interest of common sense, a unilateral program, whether it be a union member assistance program (MAP) or a management program, seldom gets the opportunity to communicate with the other side. Once a management-sponsored EAP is established, it is not likely to be later developed into a true labor-management program. Unless the union is invited to participate in the development of policies, procedures, and program implementation at the onset, the EAP will be viewed as a management program with all of its limitations. These limitations can be reduced, however, by inviting union participation at any point in time. This participation can be formal or informal. An EAP advisory committee of union and management representatives has worked well in many organizations. Even when management is absorbing the entire cost of the operation it is advisable to form such a committee. A cooperative effort will improve the EAP's potential effectiveness and prove more cost effective in the long run.

JOINT UNION-MANAGEMENT EAPs ARE BETTER

Approximately 20 percent of the American labor force is represented by bargaining agents. The labor unions serving as bargaining agents for these employees negotiate with employers on wages, working conditions, and whatever else may be in the best interest of both union and worker. Sometimes, however, these interests are in conflict with the health and welfare of the employee represented. An employee who is suspected of drinking on the job, for example, is likely to get full union support in fighting such a rule violation. If the disciplinary action for such a charge is termination, this support is seldom, if ever, compromised.

Everyone loses in these cases. Management frequently loses its case against the employee, the union must defend an employee it knows it will be called upon to defend again, and the employee loses an opportunity to take care of a serious problem. The progression of the problem is certain, deterioration of job performance is inevitable, costly grievance proceedings continue, and in the long run the employee loses the job anyway.

In joint union-management programs this will not happen. The troubled employee gets a clear message from both sides—that unacceptable job performance is not tolerated by management and that self-destructive behavior is not tolerated by the union. Many union-management EAPs exist in the United States and such programs are bound by a joint policy signed by both the chief executive officer and the union president. This cooperative effort is made clear to the union members through literature, meetings, and by distributing copies of the signed policy statement including procedures governing the agreement. Many union programs also distribute brochures to shop stewards and delegates that emphasize the importance of a co-operative program. One such brochure conveys the following message:

> Alcoholic workers often cause accidents and increase production costs through poor workmanship and absenteeism, giving industry its so-called "multi-billion dollar hangover." In addition to avoiding this "hangover," both union and company also like to avoid getting bogged down in a maze of time-consuming grievances related to alcoholism which could be prevented with a formal cooperative program. Finally, neither party relishes the arbitration costs associated with these griev-ances, money which could be better devoted to strengthen an active rehabilitation program.[3]

Joint programs have been shown to be more effective than union-only or management-only programs for several reasons. First, the program obtains greater visibility. This is likely to result in greater acceptance by union, nonunion, and supervisory personnel. Another reason cited is that joint programs are less likely to be accused of dis-criminatory practices, selectively giving employees a second chance. While this should not happen in any organization with any type of program, it remains, nevertheless, a consideration. A third reason why joint programs increase their potential effectiveness is that a greater appreciation of the chemical-dependency problem and its consequences for industry, business, and the work organization is realized. The dissemination of information to all concerned and the education process are better facilitated through a cooperative program effort. Finally, the combined efforts of management and labor, by presenting a unified posture with respect to the afflicted individual, maximize the probability of a successful outcome.[4]

CHEMICAL DEPENDENCY IS A UNION PROBLEM

Employee chemical dependence is as much of a problem for the union as it is for the employer. In one assembly plant surveyed, more than 48.6 percent of the grievances filed were alcohol or drug re-lated.[5] In an effort to reduce both the grievances and the alcoholism/drug problems in the workplace, the union teamed up with manage-ment and formed joint labor-management programs at plants where the union had employees. Many such joint EAPs now exist in the

United States and the contractual language emphasizes the human aspect of these programs:

> The Company and Union jointly recognize alcoholism [chemical dependence] as an illness which can be successfully treated. It is also recognized that it is for the best interest of the employee, the Company and the Union that this illness be treated and controlled under the existing bargaining contractual agreement. . . . A Labor-Management Program will be established for the purpose of helping the individual with this disease to recover. The program is to be designed for rehabilitation and not elimination of the employee. Any program administrators (by whatever title) will be selected with equal representation from Management and from the Union, and will be allowed sufficient time with pay to perform their program duties.[6]

The traditional role of the union delegate is to represent the interests of the employee. This includes protecting the wages, hours, and benefits of its members and insuring acceptable working conditions. But many unions also realize that alcoholic and the drug-abusing employees have been able to play their union representatives and the company supervisors off against each other so that they may continue their drinking and/or drug use without interruption. Therefore, it is essential for both union representatives and the supervisors to understand the nature of alcoholism and drug abuse. The supervisor and the union representative together ". . . hold the key to the greatest motivating tool yet found . . . " to get the chemical-dependent person to realize that he or she has a problem and to seek help.[7] This "tool" is, of course, the employee's desire to keep his or her job.

JOINT EAPs: COOPERATION VS. CONFRONTATION

While there are many bargaining chips that unions and managements use in negotiating key labor accords, the chemical-dependent employee is not one of them. Such problems become, in fact, negative bargaining chips. Not only is the alcoholic or drug-abusing employee costly to management, but also costly to the union in more ways than one. If an employee charged with an alcohol- or drug-related rule violation denies the problem, then the union is placed in the awkward position of having to support the employee's denial.

Everyone may know that the employee's drinking or drug abuse is the real problem, but there is no neutral ground on which union and management can confront the issue. The joint EAP provides such a forum and, in most cases, eliminates such problems. Frequently at the urging of the union delegate, the chemical-dependent employee gets help before job performance deteriorates to the point where disciplinary action is imminent.

In setting their differences aside and dealing with chemical dependency as a problem for all concerned, both union and management stand to win. Not only does each side benefit in terms of cost reduction and employee welfare, but coming together on these kinds of issues opens the door to discussing other problems that might otherwise call for hard negotiating. Experience has shown that the best climate in which to negotiate anything is one of cooperation rather than confrontation.[8] While having a joint labor-management employee assistance program will not end the ritual of hammering out key labor accords in marathon, round-the-clock bargaining sessions, it will demonstrate that some issues can be resolved in a cooperative fashion. In this way joint union-management EAPs benefit both the work organization and the labor union beyond the stated benefits of such programs.

NOTES

1. "Occupational Alcoholism Programs Thru Union Contracts" (Washington, D.C.: International Association of Machinists and Aerospace Workers). Offset.

2. John Brecher and Erik Ipsen, "Taking Drugs on the Job," *Newsweek*, August 22, 1983, p. 52.

3. *Alcoholism: Programs with Promise* (Pittsburg, Pa.: United Steel Workers of America), p. 18.

4. Madeleine L. Tramm, "Union-Based Programs," in *The Human Resources Management Handbook/Principles and Practice of Employee Assistance Programs*, ed. Samuel H. Klarreich, James L. Francek, and C. Eugene Moore (New York: Praeger, 1985), p. 97.

5. Alcoholism Council of Greater New York Fact Sheet.

6. "Occupational."

7. Ibid., pp. 16, 17.

8. William S. Duncan, *The EAP Manual* (New York: National Council on Alcoholism, 1982), p. 11.

8

The Corporate Culture

KNOW THE ORGANIZATION BEFORE
IMPLEMENTING A PROGRAM

The EAP, like any other work group within the organization, must find a niche within the existing corporate culture. It must fit into the existing system of shared values and organizational beliefs that interact with a company's people, organizational structures, and control systems to produce behavioral norms. Simply stated, it must fit in with what is important, with how things work, and, finally, the way things are done.[1]

In a corporation where the employee population is organized and represented by a bargaining agent, a joint labor-management EAP will be more effective than a management-operated program. Besides those reasons cited in Chapter 7, excluding the union from participation is ignoring the influence of the union on the corporate culture. The corporate culture of any organization, union or nonunion, will ultimately determine whether or not the EAP will fit in. If the concept is not accepted by those individuals within the organization who wield the stamp of approval, then the program's effectiveness will be limited. The EAP may continue to exist and even reach a small percentage of troubled employees, but those referrals are likely to be employees in the latter stages of chemical dependency. The program will be used as a dumping ground rather than a management tool to help supervisors do their job more effectively.

An EAP is not going to be effective in a company that does not have a strong corporate culture. Shared values, beliefs, and norms provide an environment that is conducive to good human resource management and that is consistent with EAP goals and objectives. The EAP concept is not easy to understand in that it takes what might seem a simple solution—firing the nonproductive employee—and exchanges it for a somewhat complicated process—treating the nonproductive employee. It places a condition on the existing progressive disciplinary procedures, adding a step that might be considered an inconvenience by some and ignored by others. Unless the corporate culture views the EAP as an important function of the organization that is not so different from other operations within the organization, the concept is likely to fail.

Poorer-performing companies with dysfunctional or no identifiable corporate culture will beget poor-performing or marginal EAPs. While an organization with a strong corporate culture will either accept or reject an idea, a weak culture will neither accept nor reject it. It will use the EAP at whim and for whatever reason prevails, usually having little to do with cost containment or with human values. Unlike those "excellent companies" described in Peters and Waterman's book entitled *In Search of Excellence*, these companies usually focus on internal politics and numbers rather than on products and people. On the operations level this translates into taking action to meet a personal need rather than to meet an organizational objective. As one corporate executive put it, "You know, the problem [in a poor-performing company] is *every* decision is being made for the first time."[2]

While the concept of employee assistance programming may be sound in theory, the existing corporate culture may render it ineffective. Unless the policies and procedures on chemical dependency become an integral part of all the existing human resource management policies and procedures, every decision to use the EAP will be "made for the first time." The decision will be individual rather than organizational.

THE MANAGEMENT FACTOR

The employee assistance program serves to facilitate and effectualize the company's policy on dealing with alcohol- and drug-related job-performance problems. The organization's motives for having an

EAP may be to help troubled employees, to save corporate dollars, or a combination of the two. The idea for a program may come out of the human resources department, the medical department, or the economic development department. Whatever the organization's motives are for considering an EAP, one fact is crucial to an effective program: management support is essential, and without it the EAP is simply corporate window dressing.

It would seem that an existing EAP would need to have the support of management for it to exist in the first place, and if it did not it would simply be eliminated. This is not always true. An existing EAP may be the vestige of the last "regime," and the existing policy statement on chemical dependency issued by the previous CEO may have yellowed with time. Any reference made to it may indeed be out-of-sync with existing norms and provoke negative reactions. Or the EAP may be in a state, federal, or municipal agency where the provision of such services is required by law. Just because the program is required does not necessarily mean that management wants it. Or it may be in an organization where the management structure is bureaucratic and any change is virtually impossible. Finally, the EAP may limp along in a democratic-style organizational structure where the management does not support the idea but cannot do much about it.

The point here is that marginal EAPs do continue to exist for an assortment of reasons having little to do with economic *or* humanistic objectives. The greatest resistance to an EAP is probably the fact that it is perceived as different from other organizational functions. This perception is based on image and language often associated with health-care agencies. Health-care agencies, and by extension EAPs, use words like "help," "sick," "disabled," "diagnosis," "treatment," and "aftercare." By contrast, work organizations "get the job done" with "efficiency," embodying "hard work," "tough decisions," and "profit."[3] The EAP is not perceived as a business management function but rather as a health-care function, operating on a not-for-profit management tract with objectives that hardly resemble those objectives formulated in the board room. This perception, unfortunately, is often reinforced by EAP staff members. Practitioners eager to communicate the human value of reaching troubled employees sometimes overuse clinical terminology that alienates both management and supervisory staff members. Most EAP professionals do not make this mistake and are, in fact, quite skillful at wearing two hats and making a transition from clinical to managerial roles on cue. The experience that allows for this transition is, in fact, a prerequisite to working in the field.

Since the EAP exists as a work-group unit within the general organization, it may be assumed that it will reflect, to varying degrees, a similar management perspective. A management that adopts organizational goals such as profit, production, and cost control, however, can conflict with an EAP staff that identifies functional objectives in terms of stress resolution and behavior modification. If it is perceived that EAP objectives diverge from organizational objectives, then management staff will not support or cooperate with the program. Of specific concern are financial support of EAP staff and programs, cooperation in personnel decisions, referrals from management and supervisory personnel, and maintenance of confidentiality.[4] This perception, however, is likely to be based on preconceived notions rather than on EAP practices. The EAP actually has two goals; one is functional and the other is organizational. The functional goal is successful treatment and recovery while the organizational goal is improved job performance and productivity. These goals are usually achieved simultaneously once the employee is referred to the EAP, but getting the employee there is part of the treatment process and this is where the resistance often begins.

Supervisory resistance to EAP utilization is an inevitable outgrowth of management indifference. Without management support of policy and program, the EAP will be underutilized and supervisors will continue to deal with job-performance problems in whatever way they have in the past. In most cases this means that early identification of the troubled employee will not be practiced and only those late-stage chemical-dependent persons will be referred. Without management support the EAP is not likely to have an aggressive supervisory training program, and without training the supervisor will not know how to address the problem.

Management indifference to policy and program leads to a corporate culture that responds to the EAP concept with: "That's not the way we do things around here." This is particularly frustrating to a supervisor who knows better and attempts to deal with a troubled employee in the "right" way, by noting the employee's deteriorating job performance, conducting an intervention interview, and making an appropriate referral to the company EAP. Unless the action is supported by *current* policy and has a firm and *current* management endorsement, the supervisor—especially a first-line supervisor—might be considered by colleagues and subordinates to be overzealous and out-of-step with accepted supervisory practices. In some work environments the supervisor may, indeed, be viewed as a "stool pigeon" or "rat" for making such a referral.

THE BEST EAPs ARE PLANNED EAPs

Some EAP advocates might defend the existence of a program in an unfriendly corporate environment with the rationale that any EAP is better than no EAP at all. On the contrary, a program that is not effective may be worse than having no program at all. A poorly administered EAP, for whatever reasons, is harmful both for the organization and for the troubled employee. Supervisory training will be nonexistent or ineffectual, research/evaluation is unlikely, and treatment may be inconsistent. Legal issues and ethical standards may be ignored, insurance plans may not provide adequate treatment coverage, and the program may actually "enable" continued drug and/or alcohol abuse rather than contain it. Most importantly, it may keep a troubled employee from getting the help that is needed.

Installing an EAP is a major decision that cannot be taken lightly. Legal details, treatment issues, confidentiality requirements, training programs, insurance coverage, personnel policies, marketing plans, outreach strategies, and program scope are some of the details, to mention a few, that must be addressed before the first referral comes through the door. In addition, program policies, procedures, training, treatment, standards of performance, productivity controls, and communications must come together in an orchestrated fashion to form an effective companywide approach to alcohol- and drug-related problems in the workplace. Regardless of the size and scope of the program, the EAP is a serious undertaking and a full commitment by management is essential to its success. While the program must also fit into the corporate culture of the organization, corporate culture is influenced by corporate management. Even in an organization where the culture is old and the management is new, the success of the EAP will depend on whether or not the leadership says, "This is the way things are done around here."

All organizations should provide services that will help troubled employees and reduce the cost of alcohol- and drug-related problems in the workplace. These services may be provided from within or contracted to an external employee assistance program provider. The concept makes sense from both an economic and humanistic point of view. But to apply the concept effectively the organization should first examine its needs and shape the program to those needs. To drop a program into an organization without first conducting an audit would be like placing a product in the marketplace without first researching the market's needs. The organization is the marketplace and the EAP is the product or service to be offered. It stands to reason, then, that factors such as employee composition, union presence, management commitment, organization size, legal constraints, and community resources be examined as the first step in planning a program. Most importantly, will the existing corporate culture accept or reject the concept? In preparing for and being aware of those hurdles that might otherwise render a program ineffective, the EAP improves its potential to function optimally and assumes a key role in the human resource management function of the organization.

NOTES

1. Bro Uttal, "The Corporate Culture Vultures," *Fortune*, October 17, 1983, p. 66.

2. Thomas J. Peters and Robert H. Waterman, Jr., *In Search of Excellence* (New York: Harper & Row, 1982), p. 76.

3. Paul M. Roman, "Barriers to the Initiation of Employee Alcoholism Programs," in *NIAAA Research Monograph 8/Occupational Alcoholism: A Review of Research Issues* (Washington, D.C.: Government Printing Office, 1982), p. 149.

4. Paul Steel, "Assessing Employee Assistance Programs: Intra- and Extra-Organizational Influences," in *EAP Research: An Annual of Research and Research Issues*, vol. 1, C, ed. Howard Grimes (Troy, Mich.: Performance Resource Press, 1984), pp. 37, 38.

9

Employee Assistance Programs Make Corporate Sense

EAPs HELP PEOPLE

The benefits and value of having an EAP can be expressed in both humanistic and economic terms. The organization's financial analyst will evaluate the program's effectiveness in terms of cost reduction while the medical director might review the quality of care provided. One would measure success in dollars while the other would see the health and safety benefits. The economic model would present the EAP's net present value while the humanistic model would argue that good health promotes good performance.

Both the economic model and the humanistic model are valid measures of an EAP's performance and effectiveness. It is difficult, in fact, to separate the two in that many of the human benefits are impossible to quantify yet undoubtedly increase productivity. Improved morale, for example, cannot be put into a calculator and goodwill has no tangible dollar value. (Actually, management accountants have a formula for determining the goodwill value of an organization.) While cost containment is undeniably a major factor in installing and maintaining an EAP, the human factor, some leaders in the field believe, is the major impetus for employee assistance programming. They interpret program benefits in human terms, showing recovery rates rather than dollars saved as proof of the program's success. *The EAP Manual* reports that managements *usually* install such programs for "altruistic reasons," and that ". . . the principal business of these programs is saving lives and by extension, families." The manual supports the notion that chemical dependency, left untreated, is a progressive, fatal disease that can be detected in its earliest possible stage in the workplace, and that an effective employee assistance program motivates the employee to ". . . accept the treatment which holds the only hope of survival."[1]

The implication here is that the employee assistance program is not intended to be a profit center. While there is a cost-benefit side to helping troubled employees, the human side is equally important. EAPs are installed to provide services for employees and their families, services that help people who are having personal problems. An article published in *EAP Digest* also emphasizes the human value of having an employee assistance program:

> EAPs have not, to date, managed to provide neat solutions to the major problems facing corporate survival, but EAPs have provided partial remedies and created new pathways for corporate considerations in terms of work life and employee health.[2]

Employee assistance programs in work organizations have not eliminated the devastating cost of chemical dependency, but they have served to reduce these costs, a subject to be covered in Chapter 10. They have also served to improve the quality of work life and create a work environment where the employee's health is an important corporate consideration. This is becoming more evident in organizations that have faced up to the seriousness of drug- and alcohol-related problems in the workplace and have implemented programs in an effort to contain these problems. Not only have troubled employees been helped through EAPs, but organizations have helped themselves in establishing a no-nonsense approach to a problem that many organizations continue to ignore. Admitting that a problem exists and doing something about it wins the respect of everyone who is potentially affected by the problem. In an organization where 5 to 10 percent of the employee population is experiencing alcohol- or drug-related job performance problems, virtually everyone in that organization is affected in one way or another. Dealing with the problem in a direct fashion reflects a corporate point of view that is both humanistic and employee-oriented in nature, and it also reflects a leadership that knows the value of human capital and how to protect that investment.

Twenty years ago few corporate managers would have considered implementing an employee assistance program that did not clearly result in a cost reduction greater than the investment cost. Now they are more likely to measure the social and political consequences of not having a program, and can appreciate the fact that employee assistance programming is a human investment that could also prove to be "profitable." Cost effectiveness notwithstanding, acknowledging the human side and not just the economic side of the EAP reflects the influence of social and political concerns.[3] The rationale that some organizations offer to defend their EAP investment, however, is quite simple: employees who feel better also perform better.

Labor-union programs are likely to interpret the program's success in these terms. The United Steelworkers guide to rehabilitation programs, entitled "Alcoholism: Programs with Promise," stresses that labor and management share common interests in helping the chemical-dependent worker, and that chemical dependency shortens life. Medical evidence indicates that the chemical-dependent person's life span is reduced by eight to ten years. In addition, this person is more susceptible to many other illnesses because of excessive drinking and/or drug use. A second cause for common concern, the guide reports, is the progressive nature of the disease. It gets worse with each episode. The prognosis is absolutely certain: illness, physical and mental impairment, early death. Another point that the guide makes is that both labor and management know the relationship between alcohol abuse and accidents. The chemical-dependent person is a safety threat to him/herself and others. All the above are important reasons for labor and management to cooperate with each other in dealing with this problem, but the major concern, the guide stresses, should be the rehabilitation of the chemical-dependent person—"to restore this person to a state of self-confidence and health."[4]

The human benefits of the EAP go beyond the rehabilitation of the employee. Helping an employee with his or her problem is helping a family with its problem. Identifying and motivating a chemical-dependent employee to seek treatment usually result in treatment for the entire family. Alcoholism or drug abuse is often referred to as a "family disease"; the chemical-dependent person is merely the "identified patient" within the family unit.[5] This person has been singled out because of unacceptable behavior, a behavior that is self-destructive and disruptive to the family.

If the EAP refers the employee to a community treatment program, the program is likely to involve the entire family in the treatment process. Most treatment programs provide family therapy for "significant others," and some even urge immediate family members to spend a short time living in the program. If the "identified patient" refuses to cooperate in the family approach to treatment, admission to the program may even be denied. Most in-patient and out-patient services are likely to be flexible on this matter.

The concept of the "identified patient" actually has its roots in family theory. It is useful to call the member who carries the symptom the "identified patient," and the identified patient's symptoms serve a family function as well as an individual function.[6] D. D. Jackson proposed the notion in 1954 that "The family behaves as if it were a unit." He used the term "family homeostasis" to refer to this behavior.[7] Virginia Satir elaborates on this theory saying that when one person in a family has pain which shows up in symptoms, all family members are feeling the pain in some way.

Hence, using the workplace and job jeopardy to motivate chemical-dependent employees toward seeking treatment has clinical implications and potential benefits beyond the obvious benefits of recovery for the individual. The EAP's value in humanistic terms becomes a geometrically quantiative measure in that it reaches several persons in need of assistance when it reaches the troubled employee. The supervisor receives assistance in dealing with a problem for which there had been no easy solution and the co-worker gets help with a problem that was at least a nuisance and at times dangerous. Last but not least, the employee's family gets help with a problem that might never have been addressed were it not for the company EAP.

EAPs SAVE SUPERVISORS' TIME

Troubled employees are time consuming. A chemical-dependent person spends a great deal of time doing whatever is necessary to continue to drink or use drugs. This includes absenteeism, tardiness, extended lunch and morning breaks, and unauthorized leaves from the work site. It also includes consuming the time of others such as fellow employees and supervisors. Supervisors who must deal with chemical-dependent employees, or more accurately, do not deal with chemical-dependent employees, spend valuable time attempting to circumvent the problem. This is especially true in work organizations where it is difficult to fire an employee. Many bureaucratic organizations such as government agencies, hospitals, and other public sector and voluntary sector work organizations fall into this group. Corporations that are unionized are sometimes locked into collective bargaining agreements and bogged down by mounds of paperwork and procedures that discourage action necessary to discharge an employee even when there is just cause. In a recent discussion I had with a middle-management supervisor about a chemical-dependent employee, the supervisor expressed frustration and hopelessness in attempts to resolve the problem. The employee was a union member who continually violated rules and regulations by committing minor infractions. Writing up these infractions would be time consuming in and of itself, but following up with the appropriate disciplinary action was even more time consuming. The actual termination of such an employee could take years. In an effort to correct the problem without bringing formal charges against the employee, several intervention interviews were conducted. The employee was counseled informally in the hope that the process of progressive disciplinary action could be avoided. With repeated failures, the supervisor's despair became evident. "If I only had the time," the supervisor complained, "I'd fire this one."

It is difficult to know whether or not the procedures are totally to blame in this instance. The supervisor, perhaps, may not have taken the time to learn what steps to take and may have been experiencing the frustration of inexperience. The troubled employee, nevertheless, can expend a supervisor's time and energies needlessly. While the EAP does not relieve the supervisor of those responsibilities that are a function of the job, it will provide continuous support in resolving highly sensitive and often disruptive employee problems, allowing more time to handle operational duties and accountabilities.[8] One important function of the EAP is training supervisors to recognize and document patterns of deteriorating job performance. With these skills the supervisor is prepared to collect the data necessary to conduct an early intervention interview. An early referral to the EAP will, in most instances, result in a positive outcome. Even if the employee does not respond favorably, the supervisor's action will be an important step in the progressive disciplinary process.

The training provided by the EAP helps the supervisor develop a greater awareness of the impact of personal problems in the workplace—the impact of these problems on morale, health, and productivity. As stated earlier, the supervisor's knowledge about alcoholism and drug abuse is not nearly as important as the ability to identify the troubled employee through patterns of deteriorating job performance. An understanding of the relationship between personal problems and work performance, however, will provide the ability to deal quickly and effectively with both troubled employees and marginally functioning employees.

EAPs ARE BENEFICIAL TO EMPLOYER-EMPLOYEE RELATIONS

An employee assistance program is an employer-sponsored benefit designed to offer employees and members of their immediate families assistance with a wide variety of personal problems. EAPs are a form of indirect compensation, a perquisite or employee service not unlike company-sponsored day-care centers, company-paid physical examinations, and social or health club memberships. Many EAPs offer legal advice, help on tax matters, family counseling, psychotherapy, and many services that an employee might otherwise pay for. While chemical-dependency services are likely to be the major function of many EAPs, providing help on other personal matters can be equally important. Having a program that addresses all kinds of personal problems eliminates the stigma of being referred to a program for alcoholism or drug abuse, and offering such a range of services changes it from a program for "those" employees to a service for "all" employees.

Employee assistance programming is simply good employer-employee relations. A program with a wide range of services that is administered in the best interest of the employee is one way to show that the company cares. The message communicated is that the organization is concerned about its people and has an employee assistance program to prove it. Providing such services is recognition that an employee's problems are also the organization's problems, whether or not job stress contributed to the problem. An employer can find countless reasons for having an EAP but few for not. From a practical point of view one reason is that the employee is a valuable resource and a costly investment that must be protected. From a human point of view, the organization is in a community that allows it to exist and has a social responsibility, therefore, to the members of that community including the employees. This responsibility is to identify troubled employees through deteriorating job performance and provide the help necessary to correct the problem.[9] While both "valuable resource" and "performance" are clearly management terms that translate into corporate dollars, this does not diminish the fact that EAPs help employees and/or members of their families—a fact that translates into good employer-employee relations.

Providing employees assistance with their personal problems reflects a human approach to personnel management that many large and successful corporations have adopted. Peters and Waterman in their report on the subject, however, assert that most companies pay "lip service" to "genuine people orientation." (It should be noted that *most* companies also do *not* have EAPs.) Identifying this as the "lip service disaster," the writers contend that:

> Almost every management we've been around says that people are important—vital, in fact. But having said that, they then don't pay much attention to their people. In fact, they probably don't even realize their omissions. "People issues take up all my time," is the typical rejoinder. What they often really mean is, "This business would be so easy if it weren't for people." . . . Only when we look at the excellent companies do we see the contract. . . . Caring runs in the veins of the managers of these institutions. . . . Although most top managements assert that their companies care for their people, the excellent companies are distinguished by the intensity and pervasiveness of this concern.[10]

Implementing an EAP will not, of course, transform an organization into an "excellent" company. The formula to becoming an excellent company is somewhat more complicated than that. It involves an orchestration of structural devices, systems, styles, and values. But it may be a contributing factor toward developing a better relationship between employer and employee. Most managements agree that their employees are their most important asset. Giving the employees a program that they can turn to for help is an action that talks louder than words, an action that will benefit everyone involved.

AN EAP IS GOOD PUBLIC/COMMUNITY RELATIONS

Good public relations is another benefit of having an employee assistance program. Many organizations have gone public with their

EAPs, boasting the fact that they care enough about their employees to provide them with help for their personal problems. *Time* carried a full-page advertisement by ITT on its EAP which was direct in its message that chemical dependency is a real and serious problem that corporate America cannot ignore (see Figure 9.1). Using a pictorial of a working man standing next to his preteenage son, the ad states, "Who does a 12-year-old turn to when his dad's on drugs?"[11]

The message is that chemical dependency is a problem that affects employer, employee, and employee's family; and that the problem exists right under our noses in business and industry. Most importantly, the ITT ad identifies the workplace as the right place for intervention and the drug abuser as a person who looks just like any other person. Finally, the ad communicates that through its EAP the company has taken responsibility for rehabilitation rather than allowing the problem to run its course, then dumping the ex-employee onto the community to deal with. Using *Time* to reach the employees of a corporation may not deliver the most efficient cost-per-thousand impressions. There are other more economical ways to do internal marketing—this is an excellent way, however, to reach the employees while at home and, most importantly, to reach the families of employees. Troubled employees often seek help at the urging of their families, and their families are more likely to take such action when they are aware of a company EAP.

The circulation of *Time* obviously far exceeds the employee population of any one company. The ITT ad then, besides being an excellent and powerful medium for providing information to employees and their families, also provides information to the readership at large. It is a form of social marketing that serves to enhance the corporate image. Unlike some companies that keep their EAPs quiet and others that have no EAP at all, ITT not only confronts the problem head-on, but tells the world about it.

Social marketing is not a new idea. It has been used by businesses and industries for decades to provide the consumer with information, usually as a public service. "Going public" with the company EAP both provides information to the general public about problems in the workplace and places the company on the cutting edge of doing something about them. The fact that chemical dependency is a serious health problem affecting business, industry, and the community is no secret. Making known the organization's effort to help the troubled employee should not be a secret either. This kind of infor-

FIGURE 9.1

Who does a 12-year-old turn to when his dad's on drugs?

hat happens to a ster with problems, the parents who ld help have problems of their own?

Like drugs or alcoholism. Or emotional crises that threaten a family's very existence.

It's hard to deal with painful situations like this at any age. But especially when you're underage.

And speaking practically, these family problems have a way of becoming business problems.

In economic terms, workers crippled by drug or alcohol addiction cost U.S. industry and society over 135 *billion* dollars a year.

That's why we at ITT created the Employee Assistance Program. To try and give constructive help to people who need it.

We maintain telephone hotlines around the world— 24 hours a day, 7 days a week.

When employees or members of their families in participating ITT companies

call us, our Program people hear them out. Then we refer them to somebody nearby who can help.

It's all done in strict confidence, without anybody knowing but the employees themselves.

A number of our people have turned to this ITT program since it began. And most are still with us, productive and happy members of our corporate family.

But more important, happy members of their own families.

The best ideas are the ideas that help people. ITT

For details, write: Director — ITT Employee Assistance Program, Personnel Dept., 320 Park Ave., NY, NY 10022. Or call 212-940-2550.

Reprinted with permission of ITT.

mation goes a long way in shaping a corporate image built on genuine concern and social responsibility.

EAPs ARE GOOD PUBLIC POLICY

Society is devoting an increasing amount of attention to the American corporation and its responsibilities to the community. "The economic functions of business are no longer as dominant as they traditionally have been," says Rogene A. Buchholz, a business environmentalist, "and they must be seen in relation to the social and political roles that business is being asked to assume."[12]

"Public policy," defined by Buchholz as an integrative concept that incorporates both "social responsibility" and "corporate social responsiveness," is becoming an important factor in the decision-making process. Equal opportunity, pollution control, poverty reduction, product safety, and, of course, programs for the health and safety of employees are public policy issues that must not be overlooked by corporate managers and decision makers.[13] Society's expectation that the private sector take responsibility for its environment and its people is expressed through sales and through the legislature. Products that are not safe are not being bought and organizations that contaminate the air are being regulated. Companies that discriminate against and/or fire alcoholics and drug abusers are being challenged in the courts. And they are losing!

Society expects work organizations to give something back to the community that allows them to exist. These "give backs" come in the form of human services that the community might otherwise have to provide, and go beyond those fringe benefits found in most compensation packages. Now industry is expected to make an aesthetic contribution to the environment, polluters are being held accountable for past and present contamination, and all business and industry is being held responsible for the health and safety of their employees. Enlightened work organizations have identified alcohol and drug abuse as health and safety issues and they are responding to these problems by implementing employee assistance programs. Providing employees help with personal problems is one way to satisfy "public policy" expectations.

EAPs HELP SET PERFORMANCE STANDARDS

Training company supervisors in the procedures of identifying and referring troubled employees is not only important to the EAP process, it is also important in setting standards for job performance and for improving operational control. Supervisors are the essential link between the employee and the EAP, and training is necessary to insure their effectiveness in this critical role. The person in charge of the unit, department, or division is trained to observe and document job performance, conduct an intervention interview, and take action on the problem. As part of the training the supervisor also learns (or relearns) the organization's policy and procedure on dealing with job-performance problems whatever their cause may be. This is especially important in large, decentralized organizations where policies and procedures may have been modified to the point where practices are not standardized and different divisions look like different companies. Training serves to reduce these differences by reinforcing companywide policy and by helping supervisors to deal with job-performance problems procedurally, consistently, and effectively. The training not only provides supervisors with the necessary skills to identify the troubled employee, but also reinforces those supervisory skills and techniques essential to day-to-day personnel management. The supervisor comes away with a good understanding of how to address all job-performance problems, including those that are alcohol and drug related.

Training is a three-hour investment of time that is especially important to first-line supervisors. Many supervisors are promoted from the rank and file and continue to identify with former co-workers. While this is an important prerequisite to the job, it can also inhibit the supervisory process. Even when the supervisor had not worked directly with those employees he or she is supervising, close identification with a troubled employee may sometimes interfere with taking appropriate action. The first-line supervisor functions in a nebulous place in the world of work somewhere between management and wage earner. Because this person is in a particularly vulnerable position, a structured approach to addressing job performance problems is necessary. As Peter F. Drucker says, "He has now, by and large, become a buffer between management, union and workers. And like all buffers, his main function is to take the blows." Drucker continues:

He is separated from the men he supervises by an ever-higher wall of resentment, suspicion and hostility. At the same time, he is separated from management by his lack of technical and managerial knowledge.[14]

While the supervisor's job will continue to be a difficult one, supervisory training reinforces performance standards and discourages judgement calls based on personal values. A clear understanding of policy and procedure, and an understanding that such problems must be handled consistently, without prejudice, allow the supervisor to do the job confidently. Objectivity, fairness, consistency, and decisiveness are emphasized in supervisory training—supervisory qualities that are also valuable in monitoring daily performance.

CREATIVE EAPs FACILITATE EQUAL EMPLOYMENT GOALS

The employee assistance program has a responsibility to reach all employee groups and provide services uniformly throughout the organization. One measure of program effectiveness is, in fact, penetration and program reach. Geographical segmentation, minority divisions, job functions, salary ranges, length of employment, age groupings, gender differences, and any number of categories forming the organization's composition can be targeted. In a corporation that has many different work groups, for example, it is the EAP administrator's job to know what the referral/employee ratio is and whether or not key targeted groups are equally represented. If one group's referral rate is disproportionately low, it could mean that supervisory training is necessary for that particular segment of the organization or that internal marketing strategies should be reviewed.

The EAP may contribute to the organization's efforts to satisfy equal employment opportunity (EEO) requirements and affirmative action program (AAP) efforts. Minority employees and handicapped employees have special needs that are addressed in any effective EAP. An effective program will develop innovative methods to insure that these groups are reached and that appropriate resources are available to satisfy these needs.[15] This is an area that had been sadly neglected in the past. In 1978 an extensive computerized search of the literature was conducted by a researcher attempting to reference information on industrial alcoholism programs for Hispanics and not one reference could be found![16] In the black community, alcohol and drug abuse problems have been largely ignored. Ironically, alcohol abuse has been cited as the number one health, mental health, and social problem in the black community.[17] Like those alcohol and drug abusers who are white, most black and Hispanic chemical-dependent people can also be found in the workplace. While more recent information shows that some gains have been made in reaching minority groups and women in the workplace, continued efforts are necessary to close the gap. Having an EAP provides an excellent opportunity to correct this problem and provides a valuable service for the organization, the community, and the employees.

EAPs PROMOTE HEALTH AND SAFETY

The EAP may also contribute to the organization's efforts to satisfy standards regulated by the Occupational Safety and Health Administration (OSHA).[18] Not only is OSHA concerned with safety and accidents in the work environment, but it is also concerned with occupational health and illness. Organizations have shown concern for the safety and health of their employees by taking steps to improve the work environment and to make employees more aware of potential problems.[19] In a recent issue of *Occupational Health & Safety*, three out of six articles addressed health problems not directly related to workplace problems, two on cigarette smoking and one on drinking. Many organizations have "wellness" programs in addition to EAPs, or distribute information to employees on all aspects of health and safety including measures to minimize on- and off-the-job accidents as well as advise on good diet, exercise programs, and stress management.

Alcoholism and drug abuse are not only issues concerning health and illness but are also safety and accident issues. The use of mood-altering chemicals is responsible for a high percentage of occupational accidents, 18,000 of which are attributed to alcohol use alone. While training supervisors to recognize and refer troubled employees is an important function of the EAP, so is educating the employee population about drugs and alcohol use and abuse. Lunch-time education programs are popular in many organizations and informational seminars on a variety of safety and health subjects are not uncommon. Many EPAs provide counseling or conduct workshops on other abuses of substances including overeating and smoking. All of these EAP functions are relevant to and supportive of OSHA concerns and objectives. The absence of an EAP deprives the organization of an important vehicle for promoting health and safety and for educating and treating employees whose use of mood-altering chemicals may not yet have reached the stage where "job jeopardy" is the impetus for seeking help.

NOTES

1. William S. Duncan, *The EAP Manual* (New York: National Council on Alcoholism, 1982), p. 11.

2. Deborah J. Comstock, "Employee Assistance Programs: Current Dimensions," *EAP Digest* 3 (May/June 1983): 46.

3. Walter Scanlon, "Corporate Cost-Benefit: Only One Cost Factor Among Many," *The Almacan* 14 (June 1984): 3.

4. "Alcoholism: Programs with Promise," (Pittsburgh: United Steel Workers of America, 1974). Offset.

5. LeClair Bissell, *Understanding Alcoholism* (Chicago: Claretian, 1976), p. 35.

6. Virginia Satir, *Cojoint Family Therapy* (Palo Alto, Ca.: Science and Behavior, 1967), p. 1.

7. D. D. Jackson, "The Question of Family Homeostasis," *Psychiatric Quarterly Supplement* (1977): 79–90.

8. "The Advantages of EAPs," *Alcoholism/The National Magazine* 4 (August 1984): 26.

9. Randall S. Schuler, *Personnel and Human Resource Management* (St. Paul, Minn.: West, 1981), p. 319.

10. Thomas J. Peters and Robert H. Waterman, Jr., *In Search of Excellence* (New York: Harper & Row, 1982), p. 239.

11. *Time*, September 3, 1984, p. 37.

12. Rogene A. Buchholz, *Business Environment and Public Policy* (Englewood Cliffs, N.J.: Prentice-Hall, 1982), p. xi.

13. Scanlon, "Corporate Cost Benefit," p. 3.

14. Peter F. Drucker, *Management: Tasks, Responsibilities, Practices* (New York: Harper & Row, 1973), p. 280.

15. Dale A. Masi, *Designing Employee Assistance Programs* (New York: AMACOM, 1984), p. 155.

16. Ibid., p. 159.

17. Ibid., p. 173.

18. John Dolan, "The Staffing Requirements of Employee Assistance Programs," in *Mental Wellness Programs for Employees*, ed. Richard H. Egdahl and Diana Chapman Walsh (New York: Springer-Verlag, 1980), p. 131.

19. Schuler, *Personnel and Human Resource Management*, p. 319.

10

Cost Benefits and Cost Considerations

SUCCESS RATES ARE HIGH

It is estimated that 25 percent of the chemical-dependent employee's earnings can be applied to the cost of lost productivity and poor job performance. It is also estimated that this employee will be absent three times more often than fellow employees, and that sickness and accident benefits will be paid at a rate three times greater than that of the national average.

The success of EAPs is indicated by the estimated recovery rates of 65 to 80 percent among employees who accept a referral for help rather than face disciplinary action for deteriorating job performance. This means that at least 65 percent of all employees receiving EAP services will be returned to "full" productivity within one year.

An estimated 70 percent of the working population consumes mood-altering chemicals ranging from alcohol to prescribed medications to street drugs.[1] It is also estimated that 5 to 15 percent of the working population are likely to have related problems serious enough to affect job performance and/or productivity.

If we assume a company with 10,000 employees earning an average of $25,000 annually and apply some simple mathematics, we can see why most EAPs do make good economic sense. Of the 10,000 men and women in the company's employ, an estimated 70 percent or 7,000 drink and/or use drugs recreationally. Of this 7,000, approximately 10 percent or 700 employees will exhibit problems related to this use and/or abuse. If we apply annual average earnings of $25,000 to these 700 employees, we have a figure of $17,500,000 paid to this group.

Taking these total earnings of $17,500,000 paid annually to this group, and applying the estimated cost factor of 25 percent (absenteeism, medical expenses, disability claims, measurable productivity losses, lateness, and other quantifiable items), we have an estimated cost of $4,375,000 to the employer. Finally, if we assume an EAP recovery rate of 65 percent, then 65 percent of this $4,375,000 loss, or $2,843,750, could be saved.

FORMULA FOR SAVINGS

$$
\begin{aligned}
10{,}000 \times .70 &= 7{,}000 \text{ drink and/or use drugs} \\
7{,}000 \times .10 &= 700 \text{ related problems} \\
\$25{,}000 \times 700 &= \$17{,}500{,}000 \text{ total salaries} \\
\$17{,}500{,}000 \times .25 &= \$4{,}375{,}000 \text{ cost to employer} \\
\$4{,}375{,}000 \times .65 &= \$2{,}843{,}750 \text{ saved through EAP}
\end{aligned}
$$

This hypothetical exercise makes lots of assumptions, of course. It assumes that replacing the troubled employee would be more costly than rehabilitation. It assumes that the 65 percent success rate will restore these employees to 100 percent productivity. It assumes that there are no rehabilitation costs involved in the employee's recovery. The biggest assumption is that this entire population of troubled employees will be referred to the corporate employee assistance program. In actuality, only 15 percent of the nation's chemical-dependent individuals are receiving some form of treatment.[2] These projections, nevertheless, serve to provide a ball-park estimate of the cost of *not* having an employee assistance program. The savings realized when an EAP is in place depend upon a great many variables. Because it is difficult to isolate all the variables essential to a "true" cost-benefit analysis, there are not more than 50 such evaluations on employee assistance programs.[3] Nevertheless, those studies that have been published all agree that EAPs reduce the cost of alcohol and drug-related problems in the workplace.

COST BENEFIT VS. COST EFFECTIVENESS

Capital investments by organizations that are in the business sector are usually made for one of two reasons: to generate profit or to reduce costs. Investing in an EAP serves the latter objective. As discussed previously, the earliest occupational alcoholism programs were products of the "new campaign for scientific efficiency in industry." The Temperance Movement, Taylorism, and workman's compensation combined to drive alochol from the workplace.[4] Two of these three influences, it can be noted, are directly related to costs and industry. Taylorism provided the first approach to scientific management and productivity measurement that associated costs and profit with time and motion. And before the passage of workers' compensation laws, an injured employee ordinarily had to file suit against an employer and prove that the injury was due to the employer's negligence. When these laws went into effect, however, the employee became eligible for compensation regardless of fault or blame. Drinking in the workplace, a problem that certainly affected productivity and costs, and was also responsible for many occupational accidents, became a serious concern to all corporate managers.

Cost containment remains an important measure of success for employee assistance programs. Whatever the humanistic value of an organization's EAP may be, a quantitative measure of the program's effectiveness is necessary to satisfy the rationale for such a program. Sometimes this is expressed in dollars saved (cost benefit) and sometimes it takes the form of employees helped success rates (cost effectiveness). The program can show, for example, that for every 1 dollar invested, 2 dollars are saved, or that for every 25,000 dollars invested, 100 troubled employees are reached. Whichever measure or combination is used, the objective is to place a quantifiable value on the EAP function. While the ultimate measure of success is cost-benefit analysis, there are other ways to evaluate a program's effectiveness. The four most widely used are: (1) A change in drinking behavior; (2) Work performance as revealed by disciplinary actions, accidents, sick and injured days taken, turnover rate, and job efficiency; (3) Cost efficiency, as revealed by direct savings for employers resulting from decreases in absenteeism and indirect saving such as increased accuracy of work; (4) Penetration rate, or the extent to which the program reaches its target population.[5]

While all four methods can be expressed in quantitative terms, (2) and (3) contain those categories of variables necessary to begin a *cost-benefit* analysis, that is, total savings/total investment costs. *Cost effectiveness* is a relative measure of success. Therefore (1) and (4) could be used in this method of evaluation, that is, total employees helped/total investment costs. Cost benefit could be viewed as an economic measure while cost effectiveness might be considered both an economic and a humanistic measure of success.

The field of employee assistance programming abounds with literature attesting to the cost benefit of programs addressing the problem of chemical dependency in the workplace. Most of this literature is promotional, estimating savings based on projected macrocost percentages. There are also several statistically significant studies, however, that show the cost benefit of having EAPs in place. The New York Transit Authority computed a savings of $1 million per year paid in sick leave benefits alone; General Motors boasts a 72 percent reduction in the dollar amount paid for accident and sickness disability benefits; and the Oldsmobile program showed similar reductions in costly alcohol- and drug-related job-performance problems.[6]

The U.S. Postal Service showed an annual savings of over $2 million through their broad-brush EAP; the New York Telephone Company claims $1.5 million and DuPont saw a return of a half-million dollars over and above its program costs. AT&T claims $448,000 in actual and anticipated savings annually.[7]

Projections of cost savings, as noted earlier, are used to determine the potential cost benefit of employee assistance programming. The actual studies cited above, and most other published reports, seem to support the validity of these projections and the notion that EAPs are sound investments for most work organizations. The average annual cost of a comprehensive in-house program is $15.10 per employee, with a range from $12 to $82.23—the latter being exceptionally high.[8] Most experts in the field agree, however, that the economic benefits are well worth the program costs. As one such expert put it, "EAPs are not cheap. But when measured against the likely costs involved in not having one, it appears to be one of the all-time bargains in the corporate world."[9]

PROGRAM COSTS VS. PROGRAM SAVINGS

In the absence of a very strong cost-benefit argument, many corporate managers might reject the concept of employee assistance programming. If it is not required by law, or does not show a net present value greater than the investment and operating costs, the

EAP, or any other such proposal, will not go any further than the circular file. Capital investments, in some organizations, must show a quick and certain profit.

The business of business and industry, many economists believe, is "... to use its resources and engage in activities designed to increase its profits so long as it stays within the rules of the game. ..."[10] The contention of such economists is that any investment activity including the acceptance of social responsibility by corporate officials undermines both the very foundation of our free society and the corporation's number one priority: to make as much money for its stockholders as possible. This point of view reflects an attitude that social responsibilities are really governmental responsibilities and that the economic measure of performance is fundamental to business and industry.[11]

With all arguments for social responsibility, corporate social responsiveness and public policy notwithstanding, many business organizations would not have any program that could not express its benefits in economic terms. In order to win the approval of such CEO's, some quantitative measure would have to assure the proposed project's economic viability; that is, the program would have to project a dollar value.

This should not be much of a problem one might say after reviewing the literature. There seems to be enough information available that clearly demonstrates the economic value of the EAP. As stated earlier, however, there is much literature and many reports on the economic benefits of employee assistance programs, but fewer published "true" research studies. And even those micro and macro cost-effectiveness studies that do exist have their limitations. They are either too specific or too general, their projections being applicable to very similar organizations or very "typical" organizations.

While any organization could commission a research group to come in and conduct a unique study, such a study would be difficult and costly. Ordering such a report to determine the potential cost benefit of implementing an EAP would be a capital investment in and of itself. Swint, Decker, and Lairson have proposed a sophisticated and precise economic model to measure the economic efficiency of industrial alcoholism programs. To apply the model, however, several economic data would be required: rehabilitation program costs, employee replacement costs averted, absenteeism cost reduction and reductions in costs of reduced productivity, sick leave, health insurance payments, and post-separation disability attributed to treatment.[12]

Some researchers in the field believe it is difficult, if not impossible, to use many of the recently developed, sophisticated cost-benefit analyses techniques. Problems of measurement, conceptualization, and requirements for extensive data, and the ". . . diffuseness of the resource allocation processes . . ." in employee assistance programs contribute to that difficulty.[13] Such a study is simply too complicated and too costly.

The corporate manager who is not convinced by the existing pro-EAP literature and cost-benefit data is also not likely to be talked into a costly unique study. Since there are more corporations without employee assistance programs than with, it might be assumed that many corporate decision makers feel this way. While 55 percent of all companies with more than 5,000 employees offer some form of employee counseling service, 45 percent, a significant minority, do not.[14] The majority of U.S. corporations, in fact, when including those with under 5,000 employees, do not have employee assistance programs and do not offer services designed to address or reduce alcohol- and/or drug-related job-performance problems. The fact that so many organizations elect not to provide such services suggests that there may be an argument for both sides. The need for a sophisticated research/evaluation model to demonstrate an EAP's current and/or potential cost benefit is, in itself, evidence that not all programs in all work organizations will always prove cost effective. For one thing, the majority of workers in America work for small companies with a total employee population of less than 500. It might not be economically feasible to install an EAP in such a company or, in fact, in any company with an employee population of less than 1,000. This is especially true where the employee turnover is not significant. A program that reaches 2 percent of its population, for example, might get 20 referrals in the first year. After that, the referral rate would be reduced to a trickle. If the company's objective is to reduce the cost of alcohol- and drug-related job-performance problems, the cost of the program and treatment costs of the troubled employees could exceed the cost benefit in small organizations. Subscribing to the services of an outside EAP contractor or forming a consortium with other small companies is an alternative to an in-house program, but the costs of these alternatives should also be examined carefully to assure the desired cost-effective objective.

One cost variable frequently cited when enumerating the economic benefits of an EAP is the expense of training new employees. Discharging a troubled employee whose chemical dependency has progressed to the point where job performance is seriously impaired means hiring a replacement. Replacement costs including training and adjustment time lost could be significant. Skilled technicians, engineers, executives, airline pilots, and any number of job categories, for example, could mean high replacement costs. But what about the other levels of employment? It could be cheaper to hire and train new employees than to rehabilitate present employees. This is especially true where the employee population is predominantly nonskilled or semiskilled. A garment-center seamstress who earns $4.25 per hour or a Wall Street messenger earning $3.75 will cost their respective companies the same $6,000 to $12,000 for a 28-day stay at a private hospital that it would pay for one of their corporate executives.[15] There are, of course, less expensive rehabilitation alternatives but the point is that such variables determine whether or not an EAP is financially viable.

All of the variable costs averted have to be measured against the costs of program implementation and operation. Replacement costs, absenteeism costs, reduced productivity costs, health insurance payment costs, and other germane costs enter into the cost-benefit formula that determines the economic value, negative or positive, of the existing or planned EAP. If a company's actual or anticipated program costs are greater than projected program savings, then the rationale for installing or maintaining an EAP must be found elsewhere.

THE DOLLARS, SENSE, AND SUM OF IT ALL

The terms "cost benefit," "cost effectiveness," and "cost containment" entered the vocabulary of employee assistance programming early on. As discussed in Chapter 3, the first programs were motivated to a great extent by economic influences, and later EAPs began to express program value through cost-benefit analyses and cost-effectiveness studies. These measures of success have served as the impetus for the growth of employee assistance programming and, in combination with those benefits that are not easily quantifiable, provide a humanistic/cost-benefit package that appeals to both "rationalism" and "human relations" models of management. Those benefits that are not easily quantified are at least as important as those that are. An employee who feels good about himself or herself will be more productive than an employee who does not. Similarly, an employee who believes that the organization has a real concern for his or her health and welfare is more likely to be loyal and conscientious to that organization. While providing services for the chemical-dependent employee alone may be appreciated by those who are helped directly or indirectly, organizations with EAPs providing a range of services are most appreciated. All personal problems adversely affect job performance, and helping troubled employees, whatever their problems are, is likely to improve job performance. In addition, these "other" services create "good will," a nontangible variable that translates into improved performance and productivity in any organization.

The value of having an employee assistance program can be expressed in many ways. Whatever methods or values are used to determine the viability of the EAP concept, the ultimate benefactor must be the organization paying for the program. In one way or another the bottom line will be scrutinized. Janet Maleson Spencer sums up her thoughts on the subject:

> In all, it seems clear that more and more employers will assume responsibility for the rehabilitation of the troubled employee as the most constructive, humane and least costly path available. In doing so, the employer at best will be able to convert non-productive employees into productive ones and at least to cut short company losses attributed to long-term tolerance of the non-productive employee by identifying those employees, fulfilling company obligations to them with respect to rehabilitation and terminating the employees who cannot comply. In the long run, these policies will benefit employers as well as employees.[16]

NOTES

1. Marvin Grosswirth, "Stoned at the Office," *Datamation* 29 (February 1983): 30.

2. "Statistically Speaking," *Center for Addictive Illnesses Newsletter*, vol. 3, no. 1 (1984).

3. Donald W. Myers, "Measuring EAP Cost Effectiveness: Results and Recommendations," *EAP Digest* 4 (March/April 1984): 44.

4. Harrison M. Trice and Mona Schonbrunn, "A History of Job-Based Alcoholism Programs: 1900–1955," *Journal of Drug Issues*, ILR Reprint, Cornell University (Spring 1981): 174.

5. Norman R. Kurtz, Bradley Googins, and William C. Howard, "Measuring the Success of Occupational Alcoholism Programs," *Journal of Studies on Alcohol*, vol. 45, no. 1 (New Brunswick, N.J.: Center of Alcohol Studies, Rutgers University, January 1984): 33.

6. William S. Duncan, *The EAP Manual* (New York: National Council on Alcoholism, 1982), p. 6.

7. Walter Scanlon, "Trends in EAPs: Then and Now," *EAP Digest* 3 (May/ June 1983), p. 39.

8. Anne Kiefhaber and Willis B. Goldbeck, "Industry's Response: A Survey of Employee Assistance Programs," in *Mental Wellness Programs for Employees*, ed. Richard H. Egdahl and Diana Chapman Walsh (New York: Springer-Verlag, 1980), p. 25.

9. Grosswirth, "Stoned at the Office," p. 30.

10. George A. Steiner, John B. Miner, and Edmond R. Gray, *Management Policy and Strategy* (New York: Macmillan, 1982), pp. 81, 82.

11. Ibid.

12. J. M. Swint, M. Decker, and D. Lairson, "Economic Evaluation of Industrial Alcoholism Programs," *Journal of Studies on Alcoholism*, vol. 38, no. 9 (New Brunswick, N.J.: Rutgers University, 1978): 1633–39.

13. Carl J. Schramm, "Evaluating Occupational Programs: Efficiency and Effectiveness," in *NIAAA Research Monograph-8/Occupational Alcoholism: A Review of Research Issues* (Washington, D.C.: Government Printing Office, 1982): 363–71.

14. Chris Lee, "Is The American Work Force Stoned?" *Training* 20 (November 1983): 8–10.

15. Current (1985) rates based on room and board plus medical and physician's expenses.

16. Janet Maleson Spencer, "The Developing Notion of Employer Responsibility for the Alcoholic, Drug-Addicted or Mentally Ill Employee: An Examination Under Federal and State Employment Statutes and Arbitration Decisions," *St. John's Law Review*, vol. 53, no. 4 (Summer 1979): 720.

11

Legal Considerations and Implications

ISSUES OF DISCRIMINATION

The Federal Rehabilitation Act of 1973 prohibits discrimination against any person with a current or former handicap who is otherwise qualified to work. A supplement was added to this important piece of legislation in 1975 qualifying the handicapped individual as a person who (1) had a physical or mental disability that impaired his or her employability, and (2) could be expected to benefit in terms of employability from the vocational rehabilitation services provided under the act.[1] This was later clarified by Attorney General Griffin Bell who concluded that "Persons suffering from alcohol and drug addiction are included within the statutory definition of 'handicapped individuals.'"[2]

The development of the 1978 Comprehensive Rehabilitation Act Amendment of the Federal Rehabilitation Act of 1973 further reduced the ambiguity in the definition of the "qualified handicapped individual." It insured that alcoholics and drug abusers who were either recovering or in treatment would be protected by the act while quelling fears that airlines and drug companies might be required to hire active alcoholics and drug addicts. The spirit of the amendment excludes those individuals whose

> current use of alcohol or drugs prevents such individuals from performing the duties of the job in question or whose employment, by reason of such current alcohol or drug abuse, would constitute a direct threat to property or the safety of others.[3]

It should be noted that compliance to the Federal Rehabilitation Act of 1973 and to its amendments is applicable to organizations that have government contracts or receive government funding in *any* form.

The implications and enforcement of this act and its amendments are best understood in reviewing a case where an alcoholic employee had been fired, *Ruzek v. General Services Administration (GSA).* In that case GSA fired the employee, a guard, for sleeping on the job. The employee appealed the action contending that the charge was related to his alcoholism, a problem he presently had under control. The decision to fire the employee was upheld on appeal nevertheless, the presiding official concluding that GSA had met its obligation by telling the employee at an earlier disciplinary hearing that assistance was available if he wanted it.

This decision was also appealed by the employee, this time to the Merit Systems Protection Board (MSPB), the administrative authority charged with adjudicating federal employee appeals from a variety of employee-initiated actions, and the following decision was rendered:

> Thus we find that, in order to afford reasonable accommodation to an employee who is handicapped by alcoholism, an agency must offer the employee rehabilitative assistance and allow him an opportunity to take sick leave for treatment if necessary, before initiating any disciplinary action for continuing performance or misconduct problems related to his alcoholism. In offering rehabilitative assistance, the employee's supervisor need not confront him with the supervisor's belief that the employee has a drinking problem, but he must make the employee aware in general terms that the supervisor suspects the employee has a problem affecting his performance or conduct, and that the supervisor recommends that the employee participate in a particular rehabilitation or counseling program which is available to him.[4]

In a critique of the case Dale A. Masi, author of *Designing Employee Assistance Programs*, concludes that the board found that GSA's "weak attempt at counseling" did not constitute "reasonable accommodation," and that the "agency should have cancelled the proposed firing and given the employee another chance."[5]

The significance of this case is that it underscores the importance of having an *effective* employee assistance program—a program that includes training supervisory personnel. First, the supervisor would have had a better understanding of the organization's policy and procedure and would have skillfully avoided discussing the employee's drinking. As the board ruling stated, ". . . he must make the employee aware in general terms" that he suspects a problem exists that is affecting his job performance. Second, the supervisor would have been trained in the technique of constructive confrontation interviewing, discussing only the employee's deteriorating job performance and offering the EAP as a means to a solution. Third, just as the incidents of poor job performance were noted, the offer of assistance would have also been documented and the employee advised that continued job performance problems could lead to disciplinary action and/or firing. If the employee's performance improves to a satisfactory level, with or without the help of the EAP, then the supervisor's problem is solved. If the employee's performance continues to decline, however, that is, sleeping on duty, then the disciplinary action could be carried out. GSA would have met its obligation of "reasonable accommodation" by formally offering the employee help and by giving him time to bring his performance to an acceptable level. Chances are that the employee would have accepted the offer, job performance would have improved, and the charge of sleeping on the job might not have ever occurred.

Janet Maleson Spencer also writes on the importance of an EAP's function and its concomitant benefits when considering the legal protection afforded the chemical-dependent person on matters concerning disciplinary action and discharge. Her report in *St. John's Law Review* states that:

> The modern view as to the prerequisites to discharge of an alcoholic [drug abusing] employee, as outlined by arbitrator Lewis Kesselman, is:
> (1) That the employee be informed as to the nature of his illness.
> (2) He must be directed or encouraged to seek treatment.
> (3) He must refuse treatment, or
> (4) He must fail to make substantial progress over a considerable period of time.[6]

Without an effective employee assistance program in place, most companies could not carry out these prerequisites before discharging an employee. Managers, supervisors, and human resource practitioners have not studied the subtleties of dealing with the troubled employee, nor do they know the legal implications involved. It is the business of the EAP to have this information and to train supervisory staff in applying it. Not only will an EAP protect the employee from being discriminated against as a "qualified handicapped individual," but it will also protect the employer from otherwise unnecessary and costly litigation. If an organization has an effective EAP it is almost assured that "reasonable accommodation" will be afforded the employee, and that the employee will have to accept the help or pay the consequences. The consequences for a chemical-dependent employee will be a progression of the illness, continued deteriorating job performance and, ultimately, termination. Fortunately, most employees will accept the treatment alternative, arrest their dependence on alcohol and/or drugs, and become productive employees once again.

LEGAL CONCERNS ABOUT EAPs

While having an EAP in place may serve to protect both the employee and the employer, it may also introduce legal and ethical issues that might not otherwise concern a corporation. An EAP could serve to reduce the chance of legal action against an employer, insuring that the company policies on alcohol and drug abuse are followed, and that the supervisors are trained to deal with such issues competently. Providing such services without *competent* legal counsel would be ill-advised, however, and could render the organization vulnerable to legal entanglement. When a work organization implements an employee assistance program and provides rehabilitation services for the chemical-dependent employee, it must also comply with federal and/or state statutes designed to protect that employee. While many organizations are not legally required to comply with such statutes, following the guidelines set forth in federal antidiscrimination acts and in confidentiality codes is simply a good practice.

The Federal Rehabilitation Act of 1973, when applicable, protects handicapped persons from discrimination while other federal laws and regulations govern the confidentiality of drug and alcohol abuse patient records.[7] These include Title 42 Code of Federal Regulations, Section 408 of the Drug Abuse Office and Treatment Act, the Comprehensive Alcohol Abuse and Alcoholism Prevention Act of 1970, and the Privacy Act of 1974.[8] Many state governments also have fair employment laws and privacy acts with varying criteria of compliance.

While any corporation might unwittingly (or wittingly) find itself in violation of those sections of the Rehabilitation Act of 1973 that protect the "qualified handicapped individual" from discrimination

(Sections 503 and 504), an organization with an employee assistance program in place may be more vulnerable. On the one hand, the EAP and the company that have done their homework will be aware of the act and all of its implications. They will be sure not to violate the employee's rights. On the other hand, any organization that is providing "treatment" has entered an arena where the litigious employee can more easily support a claim of discrimination. Not being referred to the company EAP for treatment, for example, is frequently cited in cases where the chemical-dependent employee was not afforded "reasonable accommodation" to get help. Making an incorrect assessment of the employee's problem or not referring the employee to an appropriate treatment facility may also provide grounds for litigation and/or recompense.

ISSUES OF CONFIDENTIALITY

Discrimination against the "qualified handicapped individual" might be either minimized *or* exacerbated by the presence of an EAP—depending on the program's legal savvy and the professional care by which such services are offered. As stated above, there need not be an EAP present for an organization to find itself on the wrong end of a discrimination case and in violation of the Federal Rehabilitation Act of 1973. A confidentiality case is a different matter. The federal and state laws and regulations that insure the confidentiality of drug and alcohol abuse patient records can be violated only if there *is* an EAP in place. This is a particularly important area of concern in that it applies to any service provider that "treats" people including employee assistance programs. The federal government, through both the Congress and the Department of Health and Human Services, has addressed the issues of confidential records, and it is advised that those persons involved in the administration of EAPs be aware of federal statutes and regulations governing the confidentiality of patient records.[9] Title 42 of the Code of Federal Regulations on confidentiality is one such regulation that protects patients (or the employees) who are being treated for alcohol or drug dependence.

Obviously, having an employee assistance program means opening the company's door to a host of legal concerns that might not otherwise be present. Not only does this include those discussed above, but it also includes related legal problems such as counselor negligence for which the organization may be liable.[10] Virtually any clinical decision is challengeable and any professional could end up on the wrong side of a malpractice suit. While this is not a common occurrence in the field, it should not be dismissed as an insignificant concern.

SCREENING EMPLOYEES FOR DRUG USE

Another area of concern for organizations with EAPs is the question of drug screening in the workplace and its legal implications. This is a very gray area and the legality of such practices is not yet very clear. A report on the subject published in *The Almacan* labeled drug screening as an "Anathema to EAPs, Civil Rights."[11] Routine drug screening does not sit well with EAP practitioners and firing an employee on the basis of a positive drug finding might be in violation of existing policies if the organization has a program. While a positive toxicology finding may be used to disqualify an employee if that test is used for enforcement purposes only, this may constitute a violation of the "reasonable accommodation" rule if the organization *does* have a program in place. A positive toxicology report should, in that case, result in a referral for counseling and treatment and not in termination.[12]

Further complicating the issue of drug screening in the workplace is the question of reliability of the results. The Center for Disease Control and other agencies responsible for monitoring the performance of drug-screening laboratories have conducted proficiency testing of a number of laboratories nationally. The false positive rates they actually found ranged from 5 percent to 28 percent.[13] According to a report published in the *Journal of the American Medical Association*, laboratories using urine screening tests to detect the presence of methadone, barbiturates, amphetamines, cocaine, and other drugs are "yielding unreliable results." A study was conducted based on 100 urine samples containing small amounts of various drugs sent to 13 laboratories that serve a total of 262 methadone treatment centers. The researchers reported that 91 percent of the laboratories had unacceptable false negative rates for barbiturates, 100 percent for amphetamines, 50 percent for methadone, 91 percent for cocaine, 15 percent for codeine, and 92 percent for morphine![14]

An administrative judge who is aware of these inaccuracies is not likely to rule in favor of any employer that fires an employee based on a positive urinalysis finding alone. If the organization has an EAP, not only has the employee been denied "reasonable accommodation," but the firing is based on a questionable lab report rather than on unacceptable job performance.

As for those companies that believe they are exempt from such legal entanglements because they are not actually "treating" the employee, the term "treatment" is used in the broader sense of the word. It includes assessment, diagnosis, and evaluation as well as counseling and referral.[15] This could be interpreted to mean that any qualifying organization that designates a person to work with chemical-dependent employees is providing treatment services and is required to comply with federal and/or state regulations and statutes.

NOTES

1. *The Federal Rehabilitation Act*, U.S.C. 706 (5), 1975 Supp.

2. Griffin B. Bell, "Opinion of the Attorney General of the United States," vol. 43, op. No. 12 (April 12, 1977): 3-10, cited in Dale A. Masi, *Designing Employee Assistance Programs* (New York: AMACOM, 1984), p. 167.

3. Janet Maleson Spencer, "The Developing Notion of Employer Responsibility for the Alcoholic, Drug-Addicted or Mentally Ill Employee: An Examination Under Federal and State Employment Statutes and Arbitration Decisions," *St. John's Law Review*, vol. 53, no. 4 (Summer 1979): 34.

4. Merit Systems Protection Board (MSPB) Docket SL075209017, August 20, 1981.

5. Dale A. Masi, *Designing Employee Assistance Programs* (New York: AMACOM, 1984), p. 172.

6. Spencer, "Developing Notion of Employer Responsibility," p. 701.

7. The Federal Rehabilitation Act of 1973 (Title 29 of the U.S. Code, Section 701 *et seq.*) as recorded in *Employment Discrimination And What To Do About It* (New York: The Legal Action Center, 1982), p. 2.

8. Legal Action Center, "Confidentiality of Alcohol and Drug Abuse Patient Records," in *Confidentiality*, a compilation of articles from "Of Substance" (New York: The Legal Action Center, 1984), p. 2.

9. Frank B. Wolfe III and Marthanda J. Beckworth, "Confidentiality of Employee Records in Employee Assistance Programs," *EAP Digest* 3 (December 1982): 34.

10. John T. Gorman and Lorraine C. Stapples, "Counselor Negligence and Exposure to Liability," *The Almacan* 12 (Arlington, Va.: Association of Labor-Management Administrators and Consultants on Alcoholism, March 1982): 9.

11. Dick Stanford, "Drug Screening: Anathema to EAPs, Civil Rights," *The Almacan* 14 (Arlington, Va.: Association of Labor-Management Administrators and Consultants on Alcoholism, July 1983): 3.

12. Richard C. Boldt, Staff Attorney, Legal Action Center, letter dated June 1, 1984.

13. Legal Action Center, "Of Substance" (New York: Legal Action Center, April 1984), p. 1.

14. Occupational Health and Safety Letter (April 22, 1985).

15. Boldt, letter, 1984.

12

External Employee
Assistance Programs

WHY CHOOSE AN EXTERNAL EAP?

An internal or an external EAP can be described as a cost effective, confidential, early intervention system designed to help employees with problems that interfere with their ability to function on the job. The organization's objectives in implementing a program remain the same whether the service is delivered in-house or contracted to an outside provider, that is, cost containment and problem resolution. The decision on how to provide these services, curiously, can also be described in terms of cost containment and problem resolution: What is the most cost-effective model for the organization and what model will best meet the needs of the organization?

Proponents of in-house programs will usually agree that any organization with more than 3,000 employees need not go external, that the break-even point in financial terms is far below that figure. Such a program will generally cost the organization between $20 and $40 per employee per year, depending upon the scope of the program. There are other variables, however, that the organization must consider before installing a program. One such variable is the location of these "3,000 employees." If they are at several different plants or offices, then the in-house program might not be practical. Traveling between work sites can be time consuming for both the EAP practitioner and the employees being serviced.

Another consideration is the management style and the corporate culture of the organization. That is what is important to the organization, how does the organization work, and how does the organization do things? As discussed in Chapter 8, if the EAP does not fit in, its effectiveness will be limited. A situation audit should be carefully conducted to determine whether or not an in-house program will be the most effective alternative, both pragmatically and economically. If the organization decides instead to have an external EAP, then there are essentially two choices: contracting with an EAP service center (SC) or joining an EAP consortium of cooperating organizations.

THE EAP SERVICE CENTER ALTERNATIVE

More than half of the work force in the United States are employed by organizations that have a total employee population of less than 500 people. The EAP service center (SC) evolved out of the need to reach those organizations that employ between 30 people and 3,000 people as well as larger organizations with a dispersed, mobile, or otherwise hard-to-reach work force. This includes, but is not limited to, work settings that are long distances away from corporate headquarters and employees who frequently move between geographical areas such as sales persons and transportation workers. The National Institute of Alcohol Abuse and Alcoholism makes a distinction between employees who are hard-to-reach occupational groups in terms of problem identification and groups that are hard-to-reach in terms of service delivery:

> [The hard-to-reach work force is] the universe of employed and self-employed workers, who, for various reasons, have not been (or cannot be) serviced by traditional organizational alcoholism programs; this group may include members of the dispersed work force, the mobile work force, and selected other professions.[1]

Some employees may be hard to reach in terms of both problem identification *and* service delivery. Long-distance bus drivers and interstate sales representatives, for example, can avoid early problem identification and would not benefit from the traditional "job jeopardy" model. Even when the problem is self-diagnosed the employee would not have easy access to assistance if the EAP is located at corporate headquarters. Other types of work groups such as physicians, lawyers, engineers, etc. are usually accessible but protective relationships among colleagues may hinder the identification process. Alcohol and/or drug dependence can often progress undetected to the point where these employees or professionals are no longer employable.

THE ROLE AND FUNCTION OF THE EAP SC

While the EAP service center model may not be the final solution in reaching the hard-to-reach work force, it provides a degree of flexibility and adaptability not usually found in in-house programs. Most SCs will tailor a program to the needs of the organization and provide those services that will best serve the organization's objectives. Companies with in-house EAPs sometimes contract SCs to design programs and service those work sites that are not easily accessible. Airlines, multiplant manufacturing companies, brokerage houses, and any organization large enough to have an in-house program might contract with an SC to service their branches and smaller subsidiaries.

While the range of services provided may vary from one SC to the next, the operational structure and the method of service delivery usually follow one of two models: centralized and decentralized. The centralized model will operate out of one location with all communications coming through that office. This includes support services such as developing internal marketing strategies, evaluating program performance, designing supervisory training programs, and conducting education programs for employees. The central office deals directly with the organization it is serving and all referrals, self and supervisory, are processed here. This does not mean that the troubled employee actually goes to the central SC but that a telephone interview is conducted and the employee is then referred to a local "affiliate" for further assessment and/or referral. Many centralized SCs have 800-telephone numbers to insure 24-hour service with affiliates located throughout the country ready to respond to employee needs. Sometimes called "stringers," these affiliates are generalists who are trained to assess a range of personal problems. They provide long- and short-term counseling services and know the community resources within their geographical area including detoxification and rehabilitation facilities for employees who are chemical dependent. They seldom, if ever, have contact with the employer, their function being limited to providing clinical and social work services. If the employee is a supervisory referral, a clinical liaison at the central SC monitors job performance and communicates relevant information to the affiliate assigned to the case. The clinical liaison also communicates with the employee's supervisor or corporate liaison whatever information may be necessary to facilitate treatment. This information is limited, of course, by whatever federal and/or local confidentiality statutes apply.

The decentralized SC also has a central office where much of the clinical, management, and marketing strategies are developed, but it has full-service satellite SCs strategically located to serve their geographical areas. These geographical areas might be major cities or locations convenient to client organizations. The number of personnel located at a satellite SC may vary; at some locations there may be only one or two EAP generalists present. Unlike the affiliates of the centralized model that are retained on a fee basis for services provided, the satellite SCs usually have salaried staff members who work directly with the organizations that they serve. They provide a complete range of EAP services including counseling employees, training supervisors, and conducting education programs for the employee population. The satellite SC is decentralized in that it operates as an independent EAP for the organization it serves. In terms of management structure, it is considered a separate unit for profit accounting purposes, not unlike a "strategic business unit" (SBU) or a "profit center" (PC) of a corporation.

The centralized and the decentralized SCs are also known as "long-distance external" and "local-external" EAPs, respectively.[2] As discussed above, one model directs all operations from a central SC while the other model operates locally. Still other SCs might operate as both centralized and decentralized SCs. They may have local-external EAPs in major cities but may also have an 800-number for those employees who are not within the geographical areas served. An SC that is contracted to provide services for a manufacturing firm may have a local-external EAP near the firm's corporate headquarters, for example, but must also be accessible to the firm's large sales staff. The long-distance external EAP model is added to meet this need.

THE STAFFING OF AN EXTERNAL EAP

The components of both internal and external EAPs are essentially the same. The SC must have a strong administrative component, clinical component, education/training component, and a research/ evaluation component.

The administrative component is divided into management and personnel functions. This person(s) is the business agent, the program manager, the staff supervisor, the marketing director, the policy adviser, the legal expert, the insurance negotiator, and the company strategist. The person in this role must have the business acumen necessary to communicate with subscribing organizations, be able to interpret corporate policies and procedures, understand and be able to communicate the concepts of employee assistance programming, have a working knowledge of research methods, understand clinical issues and their application in the workplace, and be capable of training and supervising trainers.

The research/evaluation component is important to an internal EAP but essential to an external EAP. This person is an expert in quantitative methods and data application. An SC might be doing a great job for its subscribing organizations but when it is time to renegotiate the contract, the proof of the pudding is in the figures. Research and evaluation are also necessary to remove those "bugs" that are adversely affecting operations. Internal marketing strategies can be monitored through evaluation and ineffective affiliates can be reviewed through quantitative and qualitative performance appraisals. Macro and micro studies are developed by the SC researcher to improve on the program's existing methods of operation and to make contributions to the field of employee assistance programming.

The educational component is the "mind" of the EAP and the clinical component is its "heart."[3] The person responsible for training company supervisors and conducting employee education programs must both understand clinical concepts and be able to talk business language. A business organization will not tolerate for long an SC trainer who comes to the organization spewing social work or psychological jargon. The supervisor needs help in dealing with the troubled employee, not confusion.

The "heart" of the SC—the clinical component—will vary, depending upon the scale and scope of the SC. Larger SCs may employ a number of EAP specialists who limit their responsibilities to one or two functions.[4] A staffing pattern could include a credentialled alcoholism counselor, a certified social worker, a clinical psychologist, and a psychiatrist, each practitioner specializing in chemical dependency.

family matters, gambling problems, eating disorders, or nonclinical issues such as legal matters and financial issues.

In a small local-external EAP, an EAP generalist might be responsible for the entire operation. An EAP generalist is a "jack-of-all-trades," able to do the marketing, counseling, training, education, and ongoing maintenance functions for specific subscribing organizations. The advantage to the generalist approach is that credibility and communication are enhanced in that subscribing companies only have one person who handles all of their EAP needs. The problem in the generalist approach, however, is that EAP jacks-of-all-trades are hard to find and training is time consuming and costly.[5]

THE SERVICES PROVIDED

The range of services provided by an SC varies with the scope of the operation and the type of contractual service agreement. There are three core functions, however, that are inherent in any full-service agreement. They include program design, program implementation or installation, and program maintenance. Program design is the developing and shaping of a program to fit the subscribing organization's needs. This not only includes the obvious tasks such as assisting the organization in developing a companywide policy and implementing internal marketing strategies; it also includes conducting a situation audit, examining the culture of the organization, reviewing existing policies and procedures, and designing a program that will complement the philosophy and management style of the organization. In this way the external EAP is similar to the internal EAP in that it is developed specifically for that organization. The program's objective is also the same: to reduce the cost of alcohol- and drug-related problems and other problems that interfere with the employee's ability to function on the job.

Program implementation is the process of moving from the drawing board to the "bricks and mortar." All program components should be in place, a policy statement will have been formulated, procedures should be operational, and SC staffing assignments have been made. Supervisory training sessions should have already begun, internal marketing strategies have also begun, and all parties should understand their role in the system. Conflicts in existing personnel policies will have been settled, insurance coverage has been determined to be adequate and, if the SC is a local-external EAP, a suitable location has been secured. If the program is long-distance external, there should be affiliates wherever the company's employees may be. The SC should be able to handle any employee crisis before the ink on the contract dries.

Effective program maintenance will follow good program design and implementation. Problems can be expected during the implementation period, but if these problems are not solved within a short period of time, then the design and/or the implementation should be reviewed. If the supervisory referral rate is low, for example, then more supervisory training sessions are probably necessary. If the self-referral rate is low then internal marketing strategies should be reviewed, or the scope of services available should be expanded.

Maintenance is sometimes described as anything that happens between program implementation and program evaluation. Evaluation is actually a function of maintenance, a function that separates the excellent programs from the sea of mediocre programs. In this age of computer warfare, a subscribing company should be able to review an SC's activity on short notice. While cost-benefit studies are difficult and costly to conduct, cost-effectiveness studies are usually included as per the contractual agreement. The difference between the two, as discussed in earlier chapters, is that although both are quantitative, cost benefit measures dollars saved while cost effectiveness is a relative measure such as the total number of employees reached, etc.

In a report on the EAP service center model, Susan K. Isenberg divides services provided into three basic categories: company services, client services, and general program consultation.[6]

Company services are indirect services, that is, all services that do not involve the troubled employee directly. These would include policy development, supervisor training, marketing plans, research/evaluation, developing a labor/management advisory committee, general employee education programs, training a company liaison, etc.

Client services are direct services or all services that are provided for the troubled employee and his or her family. These include counseling, assessment, referral services in conjunction with identifying treatment resources, involving union participation, and monitoring job performance. Also included are nonclinical services such as legal counseling, financial management, and housing advice.

General program consultation might include any limited contractual service. Assisting an organization in designing and implementing an internal EAP, for example, or training supervisors in the supervisory referral process would be considered general program consultation.

THE ADVANTAGES OF AN EXTERNAL EAP

One advantage of an SC is that it allows a smaller company to have access to a multidisciplinary staff. Where a large corporation might be capable of staffing an internal EAP with specialists, that is, family therapist, certified social worker, credentialled alcoholism counselor, etc., the small organization is likely to be limited to one EAP generalist. The generalist would assess and refer but not treat or counsel troubled employees.

Another argument for an external EAP is that confidentiality violations, real or perceived, are less likely. The SC is away from the work site, an important factor in generating referrals. Confidentiality of record is also assured since the SC rather than the work organization owns the records.

Malpractice and liability suits are avoided with an external program. The SC assumes full responsibility for treatment and case management, a condition that should be stipulated in the contract.

Other advantages include the ability to reach a dispersed population, 24-hour coverage, no vacations to interfere with program continuity, affordable full-service costs, and an improved potential for servicing management-level employees. Finally, in contracting for EAP services rather than having an in-house program, the organization stays out of the EAP business.

THE DISADVANTAGES OF AN EXTERNAL EAP

In-house programs have a higher rate of supervisory referrals. Most employees seen in-house have been referred by supervisors while self-referrals account for most employees seen in external programs. In-house program advocates argue that supervisors prefer to work with company staff while SCs claim that their supervisory referral rate is not lower but that their rate of self-referrals is simply higher.

External programs preclude work-site counseling. While on-site counseling may have its disadvantages on the one hand, on the other hand it has some distinct advantages. Not all employees seeking assistance are job jeopardy cases and many of these employees would prefer the convenience of in-house assistance.

The SC is viewed by the subscribing organization as a professional consultant, a status that an in-house program may take years to achieve. As a consultant, however, its role will be limited to those functions identified in the contract. It is not likely to become an integral work group of the organization operating within and as a part of the corporate culture.

While economies of scale usually apply in determining a fee for services, it may be less expensive for large organizations to implement in-house programs. There are many variables to consider here, however, such as accessibility of the program to all employees.

THE COST OF EXTERNAL EAPs

Fees for services are as varied as the services offered. Sometimes referred to as a "capitation fee," a full-service contract may range anywhere between $12 and $85 per employee in the organization, the top and bottom rates being extremely rare. Most larger SCs fix their rate between $25 and $55. A capitation fee of $35 for an organization of 2,000 employees, for example, will cost the employer $70,000 per year. A "utilization rate" is sometimes included in the contract and if the referrals exceed that rate, a surcharge or add-on fee is assessed.

If an SC is called into an organization for consultation services, an hourly rate would usually apply. Consultation fees could range between $35 and $150 per hour depending upon the contractual time and services agreed upon.

Some SCs may offer services on a per visit or a per service basis. If the organization is billed per employee visit, a minimum "retainer" fee is sometimes required. Training supervisors how to identify and refer troubled employees may have a separate fixed rate per training session.

SCs may be found in both nonprofit and for-profit sectors. Non-profit SCs may receive grants or supplemental funding from third-party sources; consequently, their rates may be lower. These SCs are more likely to be found serving the nonprofit sector, however, while the for-profit SCs are more inclined to have corporate business clients. Whether the SC is nonprofit or for-profit, the employer, association, or organization served is likely to pay for services rendered. Even in joint union-management programs, management is usually expected to pay most if not all costs. Employees are seldom, if ever, billed for direct services provided by the SC. If the employee is referred for treatment, however, this becomes a matter between the treatment provider, the insurance available, and the employee. If it becomes necessary for a chemical-dependent employee to be hospitalized in a 28-day rehabilitation program, for example, the SC is not responsible for the cost of this treatment.

SHOPPING FOR AN EXTERNAL EAP

Most organizations that are exploring the feasibility of contracting with a SC usually have no experience in making such an investment. While most personnel managers and medical administrators have a conceptual understanding of employee assistance programming, they are likely to have had little or no training in the field. It is advisable, therefore, that a task force be formed that includes individuals whose collective experience will insure the best possible selection. This task force should include representatives from finance, personnel and medical departments, the union, and a special effort should be made to find someone who has a working understanding of EAPs. If possible, a recovering chemical-dependent person should also be included. The task force should read whatever information is available on the subject and meet with other organizations that are subscribing to such services. Only in this way will they be able to ask the right questions and fully understand the implications of the replies.

It is essential that the task force conduct site visits. The purpose is to observe and understand how a troubled employee is processed when he or she visits the SC. In visiting one major SC, I was particularly impressed by how quickly I was ushered from the reception area to a private waiting room. The SC was apparently in the habit of protecting the confidentiality of the employees they served.

Criteria for selecting an SC falls into four broad categories: track record, product, costs, and staff.[7] It is important to learn who the SC's current clients are, what the comparative costs for comparative services are, and how the SC staff is qualified to do the job. In reviewing the types of services offered, it is important to determine which of the two SC models discussed above would best serve the organization's needs. A local-external EAP might be best for some organizations while a long-distance external EAP may meet the needs of others.

The following checklist is recommended when assessing the qualifications, competence, and potential effectiveness of an SC:

- How long has the SC been in business?
- Is it in any other business? Is there a potential conflict of interest? (One advantage of an SC is that it is its only business.)
- What are the credentials of the staff?
- How are the services delivered (telephone contact, personal contact)?
- Is there a systematic follow-up? What are the service control mechanisms?
- Will there be a good fit? Is the prospective subscriber too large or too small for the SC?
- Is there a sophisticated management information system in place? Will the SC provide cost-benefit and cost-effectiveness analyses?
- Who are the current clients? What are the turnover and renewal rates?
- What is the SC's philosophy of service? Does it provide direct services or does it assess and refer for treatment? (Direct services are included in the contract but referral services are usually paid by the employee or through insurance.)[8]

THE EAP CONSORTIUM ALTERNATIVE

Since the word "consortium" is associated with matters of a financial nature, it is appropriate that this word be used to describe organizations that come together to form a common employee assistance program. Masi describes an EAP consortium as ". . . a cooperative agreement among companies and agencies that do not have enough employees to warrant their own EAP."[9] The most basic difference between an EAP service center and an EAP consortium is that an SC is not owned and operated by the subscribing organizations whereas the consortium is. The consortium is governed collectively by the member organizations and assumes full responsibility for all services provided.

Many of the advantages associated with the SC are also applicable to the consortium. These include affordable full-service rates, a staff of EAP specialists, confidentiality safeguards, continuity of service, and a better chance to reach higher level employees. Self-referral rates are also higher in both consortiums and SCs. In addition, the consortium model is available to those organizations that may be even too small for SCs to service.

The disadvantages, however, are also similar to those of an SC. Supervisors are less likely to contact an external EAP albeit owned in part by the organization. The referral rate for employees with chemical dependency problems, consequently, may be lower than that of an in-house program.

The administration of a consortium can be difficult. Negotiating and assigning costs for services must be hammered out. While member organizations usually agree upon a per-employee rate, a dispersed employee population or a multilocation may require more servicing. The staff of a consortium must be no less skillful than the SC staff in working both with organization managements and troubled employees. The diversified nature of the member organizations presents a challenge for both consortium management and counseling staff.

THE EXTERNAL EAP IN CONCLUSION

Some observers in the field of employee assistance programming predict that 90 percent of the employee population in the United States will have access to an EAP by the year 1990. While this prediction may be somewhat self-serving, the number of organizations subscribing to the EAP concept continues to increase every year. With the majority of the workers in the United States employed by small organizations, it seems that EAP service centers and EAP consortiums have an enormous potential for growth. Also included in this market are organizations with dispersed employee populations and organizations that simply do not want to get into the EAP business. Even organizations with in-house EAPs in place sometimes contract with SCs to provide additional services or to reach otherwise unreachable employees. These might include employees not within the geographical area or employees not likely to use an in-house program.

The external EAP is an alternative to the internal EAP. It is a viable alternative in many instances and is very often the only logical alternative. The decision to go external must be data-based, of course, but so must the decision to go internal. While all the variables discussed should be considered before making the choice, choosing an external EAP is not an irrevocable decision. Some organizations, in fact, purchase a one-year SC contract to learn more about the EAP concept. At the end of that year they may decide either to renew or to apply what they have learned and build an in-house program. Whatever the basis is for choosing the external EAP, it definitely has found a niche in the business of employee assistance programming.

NOTES

1. *Target: Alcohol Abuse in the Hard-to-Reach Work Force* (Rockville, Md.: National Institute on Alcohol Abuse and Alcoholism, 1982), p. 23.

2. Ann B. Sudduth, "Assessing Employee Use of Internal and External Employee Assistance Programs for Alcohol and Control Group," in *EAP Research: An Annual of Research and Research Issues*, vol. 1, C, ed. Howard Grimes (Troy, Mich.: Performance Resource Press, 1984), p. 26.

3. John Dolan, "The Staffing Requirements of Employee Assistance Programs," in *Mental Wellness Programs for Employees*, ed. Richard H. Egdahl and Diana Chapman Walsh (New York: Springer-Verlag, 1980), p. 132.

4. Susan K. Isenberg, "EAP Service Center Model" in *The Human Resources Management Handbook/Principles and Practice of Employee Assistance Programs*, ed. Samuel H. Klarreich, James L. Francek, and C. Eugene Moore (New York: Praeger, 1985), p. 62.

5. Ibid.

6. Ibid., pp. 60, 61.

7. Howard V. Schmitz, *The Handbook of Employee Counseling Programs* (New York: The New York Business Group on Health, 1982), p. 59.

8. Interview with Hank Linden of Brownlee, Dolan and Stein, New York, June 10, 1985.

9. Dale A. Masi, *Designing Employee Assistance Programs* (New York: AMACOM, 1984), p. 61.

13

Summing It Up
and Sorting It Out

BACK TO THE BEGINNING

"The desire to alter consciousness periodically is an innate, normal drive analogous to hunger or the sexual drive," says Andrew Weil, author of *The Natural Mind.* "Drugs," the writer adds, "are merely one means of satisfying this drive."[1]

Some social scientists would take exception to such a profound statement and dismiss Mr. Weil's analogy as a convenient metaphor without substance. One does not have to look far, however, for evidence supporting this hypothesis and the premise from which it was advanced. People seek out ways to feel good—in essence, to alter one's state of consciousness—by jogging, going to a movie, sitting in a hot tub, riding on a roller coaster, or exploring the world of underwater. A cocktail, a line of coke, or a marijuana cigarette are obvious methods used to alter consciousness. Even children, three and four years old, commonly enjoy an altered state of consciousness by whirling themselves into vertiginous stupors. A few years later they may discover that hyperventilating, then having another child squeeze their chest, will product a lightheadedness or cause them to faint.[2]

The point here is that people do enjoy changing their moods even from an early age. Describing this as an "innate, normal drive" does, indeed, seem to apply when we consider *all* of the options available to the pleasure seeker. Some methods employed to achieve this objective are exploratory, others are perfectly harmless, and still others have the potential for abuse. Mood-altering chemicals—alcohol and other drugs—are most likely to fall into the latter category.

While most people who use alcohol or other recreational drugs socially do so without creating problems for themselves or others, a large minority develop alcoholism or become dependent on such substances. These individuals, and the problems created by them, are found in the community, in the family, and, of course, in the workplace. The profile of the chemical-dependent person and the choice of substances used and abused may vary from one decade to the next, but the measure of the problem's impact on society and in the workplace remains the same: human lives and economic losses.

WHOSE RESPONSIBILITY ARE THEY?

The responsibility for solving the problem has traditionally found itself squarely in the lap of the community. Employees who found themselves in trouble with alcohol or other drugs were fired and society had to pick up the cost of both shelter and treatment. The corporate sector, for the most part, did not see this as its problem. Its objective, after all, is to realize profit, not to solve social problems. Solving social problems was a function of the voluntary and public sectors, not the business sector. Some companies, however, while no less economically motivated, began to offer help to troubled employees. These companies realized, in fact, that helping troubled employees and maximizing profit were not mutually exclusive. On the contrary, the strategy was intended to facilitate this objective.

This realization marked the beginning of help for the troubled employee. First came counseling with a focus on ending active drinking in the workplace, followed by the introduction of a more formal program approach inspired by the success of Alcoholics Anonymous. The occupational alcoholism programs of the 1940s and 1950s as well as the entire alcoholism treatment community rejoiced in 1956 when the American Medical Association declared alcoholism a disease. This was an important step toward removing the stigma associated with the problem. The shift from occupational alcoholism programs (OAP) to employee assistance programs (EAP) came in 1965 when the National Council on Alcoholism stressed the importance of job performance in achieving early identification of the alcoholic employee.[3] This was an important shift in strategy that also served to diminish the stigma associated with alcoholism.

It became evident that employee assistance programming was here to stay. Industry and business had realized the potential benefits of an effective EAP and the term "social responsibility" had entered the corporate language. The mix of social, economic, and human benefits made program evaluation a somewhat flexible task. The EAP manager could demonstrate the program's value using any number of quantitative methods. A cost-benefit analysis is the ultimate analysis but program reach, cost containment, or cost effectiveness are equally valid. Or the EAP might simply be considered an employer-sponsored benefit designed to offer assistance to employees and their families.

A chronology of those factors that contributed to and influenced the growth of employee assistance programming is shown in Chapter 3. Some of these factors deserve repeating such as the Hughes Act (Comprehensive Alcohol Abuse and Alcoholism Prevention, Treatment and Rehabilitation Act), which provided federal funding for state programs. It made the concept of employee assistance programming a public policy issue. Other influences are difficult to chronicle. The coming together of union and management in forming joint programs, for example, is an attitude rather than an event, acknowledging chemical dependency as a problem of concern to all and influencing a cooperative effort to resolve the problem.

Special interest groups of Alcoholics Anonymous such as lawyers' groups, physicians' groups, and intervention groups for airline pilots made it easier for reticent work organizations to admit that they too have employees with chemical dependency problems. Politicians, presidents' wives, actors and actresses, sports heroes, and rock stars have brought chemical dependency out of the closet, emphasizing the importance of treatment and underscoring the success of rehabilitation efforts. Even insurance companies are gradually, but slowly, expanding their coverage to include the treatment of alcoholism and drug abuse.

The corporate community has responded to date with approximately 8,000 employee assistance programs serving millions of employees throughout the United States.[4] In addition, there are other alternatives to in-house programs such as joining an EAP consortium of smaller companies that subscribe to an existing service or contracting with an EAP consultant or EAP Service Center.

THE ORGANIZATIONS THAT DO

The value and benefits of employee assistance programming are documented throughout this text. Terms most used to express these values include cost containment, improved employee relations, high morale, cost benefit, recovery, occupational health and safety, humanistic concerns, corporate social responsiveness, family benefits, and improved job performance. While there are few, if any, negative concerns in a well-administered EAP, there are several planning considerations. They include but are not limited to program cost, organizational structure, corporate culture, organization size, legal constraints, and union input if applicable.

Some corporations, the literature suggests, provide such services for "altruistic reasons."[5] Others look for a positive dollar value, viewing the EAP as a work group that will prove its worth in economic terms. Many organizations believe it to be their social responsibility to provide such services and still others consider it an investment in human capital.[6] Most organizations with EAPs in place would probably agree, however, that their rationale for offering such services is a mix of all of the above.

The employee assistance program also serves to encourage a human relations approach to human resource management. It opens the door to a management style that benefits both employer and employee. It is a human approach to a costly problem that can work effectively in any organization if administered properly. This is not to say that a corporation will or should abandon its "rationalism" management style and adopt a human relations management style.[7] The EAP is, in fact, a rational approach to a serious problem that is most effective in such organizations. The benefits of an EAP—both economic and humanistic—can be realized even in a company that adamantly defends the position that its only objective is to make as much money as possible for its stockholders ". . . so long as it stays within the rules of the game. . . ."[8] The fact notwithstanding that society has tightened these rules, the cost-reducing benefits of an EAP may actually facilitate that objective.

The EAP's objective is to help troubled individuals with their problems and return them to the job as full functioning employees. This transition can take place on all levels of the organization and may include union or nonunion workers, line or staff employees, management or nonmanagement personnel. In the process of achieving this goal the EAP makes other contributions to the organization. It helps set standards of behavior and provides guidelines for management and supervisory staff to carry out these standards. Policies are established to deal with the problems associated with chemical abuse in the workplace and procedures are formulated to deal with those employees whose job performance has been affected by alcoholism and/or drug dependence. The EAP is more than a service for troubled employees. It is a work group within an organization that shapes human resource management policy and strategy. The scope of the problem and the cost to the employer make chemical dependency a management issue with a high priority. The advocate for employee assistance programming can argue the benefits of the EAP ad infinitum. It promotes well-articulated policies and standards on drug and alcohol use and abuse, as well as on other troubled-employee problems affecting job performance. Supervisors and managers are trained to address these problems appropriately, gaining confidence and credibility in their role. Lost productivity, absenteeism, and poor job performance are reduced and troubled employees become productive employees. Sharp reductions in tardiness, long lunches, and early quitting incidents are likely. Reductions in on- and off-the-job injuries as well as in the number of disability claims and compensation applications filed have been reported. Reduced insurance premiums and/or payments for employee medical expenses are realized. Employer-employee relations are improved and a human relations management approach is fostered. Charges of discrimination against the "qualified handicapped individual" are avoided. Concern for the employee's health and welfare is demonstrated and improved union-management relations are likely. Employee education programs on drinking, drug use, and related issues are conducted. A companywide awareness of chemical dependency as a health problem is adopted and rehabilitation as an alternative to firing is realized.

THE ORGANIZATIONS THAT DO NOT

The company employee assistance program's benefits are both direct and indirect, quantified and qualified, economic and humanistic. The program's value extends to the community, the family, and to society. Society at large stands to benefit when the corporate sector takes care of its own. Yet many organizations choose not to address drug- and alcohol-related problems in a systematic or programmatic way. One reason may be that they have not yet learned about EAPs and the value of their function. Or, perhaps, the potential benefits may be known but no one has taken the bull by the horns and proposed the idea to management. Some corporate managers may be repelled by the suggestion of an EAP, maintaining the illusion that no such problems exist in their organization. Other corporations may practice a management style that leaves no room for clinical solutions to problems that, in management's view, call for disciplinary action. An autocratic management style, for example, may preclude the fruition of any such proposal unless, of course, the idea is that of the autocrat's.

Some organizations may have difficulty in getting such proposals over all the bureaucratic hurdles that they never get beyond the idea stage. Still others may not be "enlightened" to chemical dependency as a health problem and hold to the notions that alcoholism is a character weakness and drug abuse is a criminal activity. Many organizations are simply so poorly managed that chemical dependency in the workplace is the least of their problems.

Some organizations have, undoubtedly, examined the pros and cons of employee assistance programming, concluding that the payoff would not justify the investment; that the EAP with all of its concomitant benefits would not improve upon their existing practices and procedures for addressing such problems. From a cost containment point of view, it might be cheaper to fire than to rehabilitate employees. This may be especially true where the employees are unskilled, or where the capital investment tied up in an EAP might realize a better return somewhere else. Small companies may rule out the concept as not cost effective.

Finally, some corporations do not wish to get into the treatment business. Confidentiality requirements and ethical and professional standards must be adhered to and counselor negligence and exposure to liability are realistic concerns.

A PROBLEM THAT WILL NOT QUIT

Whatever the motives for installing an EAP or the rationale for not, history tells us that alcoholism and drug-related problems in the workplace will continue to be a growing concern. The trend shows increased usage and certainly a greater variety of mood-changing substances available in today's society. There are millions of employed individuals whose job performance and productivity are adversely affected, and their progressive dependence on drugs and/or alcohol will result in termination and even early death if left untreated. The cost to business and industry is billions of dollars annually, a cost ultimately passed on to the consumer.

Some authorities in the field of employee assistance programming describe the problem of chemical dependency as reaching epidemic proportions. Alcohol use remains at a relatively constant rate, but the growing use of other mood-altering drugs has created special problems for the corporate manager and challenges for the traditional EAP. Legal, ethical, cost, and policy considerations are discussed in organizations both with programs and without programs. Those organizations with programs in place, however, are in a position to manage the problem in a planned, systematic, and professional fashion while those without EAPs practice reactive management. There are good arguments for and against the EAP and most organizations can defend their position whatever it is. The needs and objectives of the organization and the variables plugged into the decision matrix will support their position. A company with 1,000 employees, for example, can easily demonstrate that an EAP would not prove cost effective. Those employees reached and returned to full productivity would not justify the investment costs. If the same company applied the human capital theory principle instead of cost-benefit analysis, however, it may reach a different conclusion, that is, the EAP as an employee benefit that generates an income stream greater than the investment cost.[9] Alternately, it can implement an external program rather than an in-house program—as discussed above, EAP consultants, EAP service centers, and EAP consortiums are ideal for small organizations.

THE EAP AS A MANAGEMENT FUNCTION

The growth of employee assistance programming over the last four decades is attributed to the positive results as perceived by the employer. The early occupational alcoholism programs demonstrated that the workplace is the right place to address alcohol-related job-performance problems. The EAP concept picked up greater momentum after discovering that the alcoholic could be reached earlier if job performance became the criteria for referring a troubled employee to the EAP. This changed the supervisor from a diagnostician back to a supervisor. The supervisor no longer had to look for symptoms of alcoholism but looked for an expected measure of performance. This same method is used to identify drug abusing employees and offer them an opportunity to seek help through the company EAP.

From an economic point of view that concept appears to work well. The employee keeps the job and continues to earn a living while the employer keeps the employee and continues to earn a profit. This assumes, of course, that the employee responds to the help being offered. Unfortunately, this is not always the case. Some employees will be terminated because they refuse to cooperate with the EAP, or because they continue to relapse even with the help offered, or because their job performance does not improve even after rehabilitation. This is employee-response failure (ERF).

From a systems point of view the concept also appears to work well. The EAP trainer or counselor shows the supervisor how to observe the troubled employee, how to document deteriorating job performance, how to conduct a constructive confrontation, and how to refer the employee to the EAP for help. The supervisor also learns how to be objective, fair, consistent, and decisive in addressing such problems and in dealing with all employee job-performance problems. The counselor advises the supervisor to call any time for assistance, serving as a consultant on specific cases. The only referrals the EAP gets, however, are late-stage alcoholics, and the only phone calls received are from supervisors who want to know how to "get rid of the drug addicts." This is supervisor-response failure (SRF).

From an operational point of view, the EAP seems to have what it needs. The clinical, educational, and program evaluation components are in place (all these functions are often handled by one person). Counseling is taking place, the training potential is there, and statistics are being kept to determine the program's effectiveness. But management has not taken any particular position on alcoholism and/or drug abuse, and no policy statement from the CEO has been issued. The EAP is a low-level operation and procedures on program utilization are usually ignored by supervisory personnel. The program function has not been integrated into existing personnel policies and procedures. This is management-response failure (MRF).

Employee-response failure will happen in the best of programs. An EAP that functions on a management level and is efficiently and effectively administered will report a certain percentage of failures. Like individuals suffering from any illness, some chemical-dependent persons will relapse and others may not respond to treatment at all. Supervisor-response failure and management-response failure, however, are somewhat controllable. SRF is, in fact, directly related to MRF. While SRF could be a symptom of a dysfunctional corporate culture, it can also reflect management's indifference or ambivalence to both the problem and the solution. Unless the procedures for dealing with the troubled employee are a function of official personnel policy, the supervisor will not take the trouble to read these procedures, no less follow them. The EAP's efforts to effect a systematic approach to the chemical-dependency problem will be politely tolerated, but a lack of managerial clout will render these efforts ineffective.

As discussed in earlier chapters, several factors may affect the effectiveness of an EAP. The employee assistance program coordinator is responsible for orchestrating a system of functions that will assure optimal effectiveness. But unless the coordinator position is on a management level, the program's success will be limited. The EAP operation must have the same opportunity to communicate its needs to top management as do other work groups within the organization, that is, finance, public relations, and production departments. This communication begins with a policy statement from the CEO but does not end there. Chemical dependency is a costly corporate problem that deserves a place in the strategic planning process. It should be an important consideration when developing tactical strategies to reduce the cost of staying in business. The level on which the EAP functions will determine its input into this process and, ultimately, its importance and credibility within the organization.

Chemical dependency in the workplace is a pervasive and insidious problem which is not likely to disappear without a planned course of action. Taking no action is, in a sense, a decision to tolerate alcoholism and drug abuse as long as the employee can get away with it. This means that the organization will ignore the problem until job performance deteriorates to the point where the employee is no longer functioning and termination is inevitable. The organization may even have a written policy on dealing with alcohol and drug use on the job administratively but without provisions for treatment and rehabilitation. Random urine samples might be taken from employees, and employee lockers might be routinely searched for contraband. Some organizations even have dogs trained to find drugs and drug paraphernalia. While this approach is likely to keep drugs and alcohol out of the workplace, it addresses only the tip of the iceberg. The lion's share of the cost of chemical dependency to business and industry is incurred not by this group of employees, but rather by those troubled employees who have not yet reached the point where drinking and/or drug use is that obvious. Many can "control" their consumption, avoiding the use of mood-altering substances during working hours. Their deteriorating job performance, however, cannot be controlled and this is what we attribute the "multi-billion dollar hangover" to.

Attempting to mandate a chemical-free employee population using these methods alone is not realistic and is out of touch with current management trends. Not only does it not fit into the human relations approach to management, but it does not fit into the rational-economic management model either. Managing alcohol- and drug-related problems in the workplace has two equally important parts. One part is a firm policy and enforceable penalties for employees who violate rules on use and/or possession of alcohol and/or drugs on the job. The second part is a policy and procedure for helping troubled employees with problems that interfere with their ability to function on the job. Choosing to manage one part and not the other is like choosing to manage only half of the organization's investments. The other half is, in fact, responsible for the greater share of those costs associated with the "multi-billion dollar hangover." Like that part of the iceberg that is under water, this is the part that should not be ignored.

While the absolute cost of chemical dependency to the organization might be hidden under various categories, the effects of the problem on human resource management, employer-employee relations, and corporate morale cannot be hidden. Yet most companies have neither formulated a workable policy on chemical dependency nor implemented an EAP. Some, perhaps, never will. Nevertheless, the concept remains a dynamic approach to a serious problem affecting industry and business. Increasingly, the issue discussed by management today is not whether to implement an EAP, but rather how to go about doing it.

STEPPING UP TO AN EFFECTIVE PROGRAM

The EAP's design and functions have been discussed in previous chapters and this section will not be a detailed recap of that information. Since form follows function, however, a step-by-step reconstruction of the EAP system seems in order (see Figure 13.1). This system is an integration of functions and responsibilities that evolve one step at a time. The first step is *designing the EAP system.* This involves determining what will be necessary to meet the organization's basic needs. The intended scope of the program and the size of the organization will determine the number of EAP staff members necessary to do the job, and the disciplines from which they should be recruited. An EAP in an organization that has employees throughout the country will be designed differently from a program serving one location. An external EAP might be contracted to serve work locations not accessible by the in-house EAP. The physical location of the program as well as the organizational level of functioning are equally important to the program's success. The union(s), where applicable, should be invited to participate, and an advisory committee of labor and management representatives formed to govern operations. Community treatment resources and insurance coverage must be secured before the first referral is made to the EAP. The design of the EAP should facilitate an interfacing of management, union, and employee population with the program, and the program with the community resources necessary to the success of the system. The EAP, like any other capital investment, should be researched, planned, and designed to insure optimal effectiveness and efficiency.

The organization must *formulate policy and procedures* if it expects to do the job right. A policy statement from the CEO is essential, confidentiality requirements must be established, and procedures for program utilization should be available. This is the single most important task in that it governs the entire system and protects all involved.

Supervisory training is critical to the EAP's success. As discussed in earlier chapters, it is not as important for the supervisor to understand chemical dependency as it is to know how to make a referral to the EAP. On-site training sessions should be planned and conducted on a regular basis and procedures should be distributed to all supervisory personnel.

FIGURE 13.1. Constructing the EAP

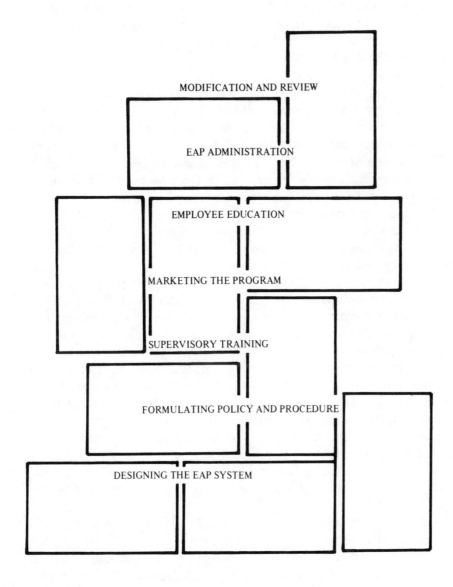

MODIFICATION AND REVIEW

EAP ADMINISTRATION

EMPLOYEE EDUCATION

MARKETING THE PROGRAM

SUPERVISORY TRAINING

FORMULATING POLICY AND PROCEDURE

DESIGNING THE EAP SYSTEM

Source: Compiled by author.

Marketing the program means more than advertising the program. The objective of any marketing effort is to, ultimately, actualize an exchange between the service provider and the prospective client. In this case the EAP is the provider and both the employees and the supervisors are the clients. In order for these clients to "buy" the EAP services, these services must fulfill a need. It is essential, therefore, that the EAP know what these needs are, and offer whatever is necessary to meet them. It is equally important that the employee population and the supervisory staff learn what their own needs are. Through education and training this is accomplished and the need for services is "created." The EAP is then ready to use whatever media are available to promote the services offered.

Employee education, as suggested above, is an important step in constructing an EAP. The employees learn that the EAP is an employer-sponsored benefit designed to offer a variety of services for employees and their family members. As the program gains acceptance among the general employee population, the number of self-referrals increases and a level of trust is established. This makes it easier for the supervisor to make a referral and for the troubled employee to accept a referral.

EAP administration is managing all the functions and responsibilities of the program. This includes maintaining an organizational position conducive to fulfilling the EAP's objectives, insuring that there is adequate insurance coverage for employees needing treatment, implementing and maintaining a record-keeping system, maintaining malpractice liability insurance, and hiring a qualified EAP staff. The administrator must also review existing personnel policies and attempt to eliminate any conflicts. In a small EAP the counselor, the trainer, and the administrator may be the functions of one person.

Modification and review allow the EAP to develop and change as needs change for both the organization and the program. Research and evaluation are functions of this process and, based on available data, the program is shaped to provide the best future outcomes. This includes success rates as well as program reach within the organization. Community resources and treatment approaches are scrutinized, and program modifications are made that best serve both employee and employer. Because objectivity is important here, an advisory committee may enhance the utilization and review process.

THE EAP IS A SYNERGISTIC FUNCTION

The employee assistance program is the single most effective approach to reducing alcoholism and drug abuse in our society. It is a conduit to the best of treatment resources available, using the threat of job loss as a lever to encourage treatment as an alternative to continued chemical abuse and dependency. In using the job as a treatment tool, the employer precipitates a crisis that the troubled employee must attempt to resolve. Most employees will accept the EAP alternative rather than risk disciplinary action and termination.

Electing to install a company EAP is a decision that is easy to justify. Most programs can demonstrate a positive cost-benefit ratio using sophisticated analysis methods and many more can prove cost savings using estimates and projections. Going beyond such finite measures of success, the EAP's value can also be expressed in humanistic, political, and social terms. An EAP providing a range of services for employees and their families is an invaluable asset both to the community and to the company.

There are countless opportunities for an individual in the world of work that do not exist for those who are unemployed. Not only is it a place where the means to survive are secured, but it is also a place where social needs, personal ambitions, and individual achievements are realized. In a ranking of what employees most want from their jobs, a "sympathetic understanding of personal problems" scores a high third, only behind a "full appreciation for work done," and "feeling 'in' on things." "Good wages," surprisingly, ranked fifth and "tactful disciplining" ranked tenth![10]

Among other things, one could conclude from these findings that there is a basic need to feel secure ("appreciation" and "feeling in"), followed by a need for assistance when one is feeling insecure ("sympathetic understanding"). Is it any wonder, then, that the EAP in helping employees solve personal problems would be especially successful when these personal problems are affecting job security? Chemical dependency is one such problem and the solution to the problem, both for the employer and the employee, can be found right in the workplace. The supervisor and the EAP counselor form a team effort that places the employee on notice while providing an opportunity to get help. The team is, in a sense, threatening to take away the employee's means of support if assistance is not accepted and job performance does not improve. Ironically, the threat of job loss becomes humanistic when that threat is instrumental in treatment and recovery.

The organizational value of the EAP is synergistic. The threat of job loss and the availability of help for personal problems each have separate values. But it is the combination of these separate values that provides a powerful tool serving organizational objectives. It is here that two different systems come together to solve both the economic and human costs of chemical dependency and other personal problems. One system's objective is behavior modification and stress management while the other system's objective is cost containment and productivity. The EAP is a combination of these objectives, restoring the troubled employee both to full health and full productivity. In a well-administered program there will never be a conflict because the bottom line will always be the employee's job performance. The organization's objective in installing an EAP is, after all, to reduce the cost of personal problems affecting job performance. While "altruism," "humanism," and "concern" should not be dismissed as having no place in organizational management, the EAP's objectives are the objectives of the organization. These objectives are, in fact, both functional and pragmatic. Harrison M. Trice must have had this in mind when he wrote:

> EAPs are an expression of humane pragmatism. The EAP does its best job for the corporation, society and the individual when it abjures the soul-saving posture and is faithful to its definition as primarily an organization strategy to keep the competent worker working.[11]

NOTES

1. Andrew Weil, *The Natural Mind* (Boston: Houghton Mifflin, 1973), p. 19.
2. Ibid.
3. *Target: Alcohol Abuse in the Hard-to-Reach Work Force* (Rockville, Md.: National Institute on Alcohol Abuse and Alcoholism, 1982), p. 3.
4. Betty Ready, "ALMACA's Membership Problem," *The Almacan* 14 (April 1984): 3.
5. William S. Duncan, *The EAP Manual* (New York: National Council on Alcoholism, 1982), p. 11.
6. Carl J. Schramm, "Evaluating Occupational Programs: Efficiency and Effectiveness," in *NIAAA Research Monograph–8/Occupational Alcoholism: A Review of Research Issues* (Washington, D.C.: Government Printing Office, 1982), p. 368.

7. Thomas J. Peters and Robert H. Waterman, Jr., *In Search of Excellence* (New York: Harper & Row, 1982), p. 29.

8. George A. Steiner, John B. Miner, and Edmund R. Gray, *Management Policy and Strategy*, 2nd ed. (New York: Macmillan, 1982), p. 81.

9. Schramm, "Evaluating Occupational Programs," p. 368.

10. Paul Hersey and Kenneth H. Blanchard, *Management of Organizational Behavior: Utilizing Human Resources*, 3rd ed. (Englewood Cliffs, N.J.: Prentice-Hall, 1977), p. 47.

11. John McVernon, "Defining the Perimeters of EAP," *The Almacan* 14 (April 1984): 8.

Index

absenteeism, 1, 97

administrative: component of EAP, 63; functions of EAP, 61–62

affirmative action. *See* equal employment opportunity

Alcoholics Anonymous: first of self-help groups, 14; influence on OAP development, 22; as pivotal point in treatment, 14

alcohol use and alcoholism: Bensinger, Peter B., report on, 2; cost and scope of, 1–3, 96; costs, non-quantified, 2; defined, 8–10; first drink experience, 10–11; Industrial Alcoholism Institute report on, 2; NCA report on, 2; in the nineteenth century, 21; productivity affected by, 96–97; and women, 39. *See also* chemical dependency; chemical-dependent person; drug use and abuse

benefits. *See* fringe benefits; employee assistance programs, benefits and value of

black employees, 7. *See also* equal employment opportunity)

chemical dependency: a corporate problem, 3; cost and scope of, 1–3; duel, 6; and EAPs, 17; a growing concern, 3; history of, 5; and job performance, 17–18. *See also* alcohol use and alcoholism; chemical-dependent person; drug use and abuse

chemical-dependent person: misconceptions about, 38–39; profile of, 7–8; responsibility for, 127; rate of consumption by, 96; stereotyping, 38; treatment of, 14–15; as a union member, 33; vs. the alcoholic employee, 25; Washton, Arnold M., report on, 8. *See also* alcohol use and alcoholism; chemical dependency; drug use and abuse

clinical component of EAP, 64

cocaine: hotline on, 7; recreational use of, 10; study on, 7–8; use in Coca Cola and tonics, 12; user profile, 7–8; women and, 3

Code of Federal Regulations, 109

Comprehensive Alcohol Abuse and Alcoholism Prevention Act of 1970, 108

Comprehensive Rehabilitation Act Amendment. *See* Federal Rehabilitation Act of 1973

confidentiality: issues of, 109–10; laws on, 26; of records, 64; and standards, 58; and trust, 46–47

consciousness, altering of: methods used in, 126–27; *The Natural Mind* on, 11–12; Weil, Andrew on, 11–12

consortium, EAP: advantages and disadvantages of, 124; as an alternative for small organizations, 101–2, 123; in sharing a central EAP, 57; vs. a service center model, 123. *See also* external employee assistance programs; service centers, EAP

About the Author

WALTER F. SCANLON, MBA, CAC has fifteen years experience in the fields of chemical dependency and employee assistance programming. This experience is both clinical and administrative including positions as director of program and marketing operations for The Freeport Group, EAP Coordinator for the Port Authority of New York and New Jersey, and residential facility director for the Beth Israel Medical Center Alcoholism Treatment Program, New York City.

Mr. Scanlon has published articles on marketing health care services, employee assistance programming, and public relations. He serves as chairperson of the editorial committee for the New York City Chapter of the Association of Labor-Management Administrators and Consultants on Alcoholism.

Mr. Scanlon holds a Bachelor of Professional Studies from Pace University and a Master of Business Administration from the New York Institute of Technology.